American Waterfowl

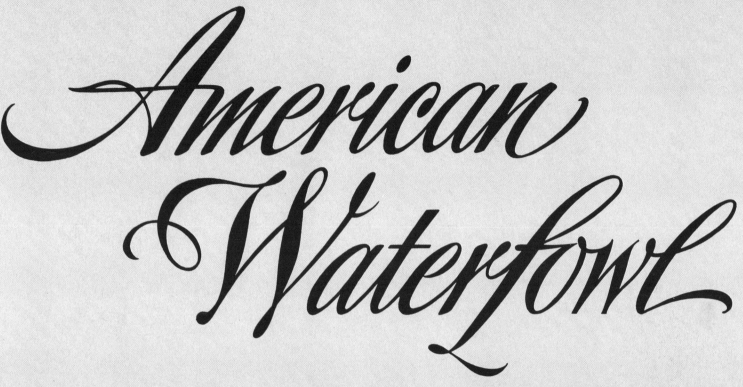

American Waterfowl

THE FEDERAL AND FIRST-OF-STATE DUCK STAMPS AND PRINTS

Introduction by Michael Ruscoe

HUGH LAUTER LEVIN ASSOCIATES, INC.

Distributed by Macmillan Publishing Company.

Printed in Italy by Gruppo Editoriale Fabbri, S.p.A. Milano.
© 1989 Hugh Lauter Levin Associates, Inc., New York

ISBN 0-88363-489-9

INTRODUCTION

In the last half-century, federal and state duck stamps and prints have taken their place among the most popular American collectibles. As investments, duck stamps are about as close to "a sure thing" as collectors can get. Stamps and prints are often valued and sold at hundreds of times their original issue price; a collection of federal stamps with their accompanying prints from 1970 to 1987, purchased for about $1200, can now be sold for as much as $40,000. Based on works by some of the country's finest wildlife artists, the stamps and prints are, moreover, beautiful artistic creations. And the money raised by duck stamp purchases (and in state programs, money raised by print purchases as well) is used exclusively for the preservation of American wetlands. Since this benefits not only waterfowl, but myriad species of wildlife that inhabit wetlands across the country, duck stamps and prints are extremely popular among collectors who would have their money go towards the protection of the environment.

Among duck stamp collectors, there are no stamps and prints more desirable than the federal and first-of-state editions. The federal program, the first of its kind, is the model on which all other wildlife stamp programs are based. The annual release of the federal stamp is a major event for duck stamp aficionados. The federal design competition itself draws hundreds, and sometimes thousands, of entries each year, and the winner reaps a fortune through the sale of prints based on his or her design.

The emergence of the state stamp programs has represented a series of milestones for collectors. Each time a state initiates a program, it gives the collector a chance to get in on the "ground floor" of a new series of stamps and prints. With more and more stamps being issued, states are faced with the challenge of putting ever-new and fresh designs before the public, and quality remains high. Thus, "first-of-state" stamps, as they are called, occupy a special place in any duck stamp collection.

Duck stamps are limited-edition stamps that are required by law to be affixed to the license of anyone wishing to hunt waterfowl. The federal government, in passing the Migratory Bird Hunting Stamp Act in 1934, required that anyone who wishes to hunt ducks, geese, or swans must be 16 years of age or older and carry a current duck stamp on which his or her signature appears.

Funds raised by the sale of federal duck stamps must be placed into the Migratory Bird Conservation Fund. This money is used by the U.S. Fish and Wildlife Service, a branch of the Department of the Interior, for the purchase, development, and maintenance of federal wildlife refuges. A percentage of the money raised through stamp sales is also used for stamp printing and distribution, enforcement of the act, and administrative costs. All but twenty-two cents of every $10 spent on the stamp (the price of the stamp rises to $12.50 for the 1989–90 edition) is used for the purchase of wetlands.

In the 1970s, beginning with California in 1971, states began forming their own stamp programs to provide millions of dollars for the acquisition and preservation of in-state wildlife refuges and to educate hunters by requiring them to put something back into the maintenance of the refuges that they use.

Duck stamp prints are full-sized editions of the designs chosen for the duck stamps. For many people, these prints are the finest art collectibles in America.

As implied above, federal and state programs differ with regard to prints. Winning artists in the federal duck stamp competition retain the publishing rights for prints, and as a result they have earned as much as a million dollars in print sales. Part of the revenue generated by state print sales, however, is withheld by the states. In 1986, Congress debated changing the federal policy, but the proposed bill never passed from committee review to final legislation.

History of the Federal Program

The federal duck stamp program and, in turn, each state program, owe their existence to one man who had the foresight to cherish American wildlife before it had the chance to disappear: Jay Norwood Darling. It was Darling's environmentalism and artistic talent that merged to form the concept of duck stamps.

Darling was introduced to the outdoors by his father, a Congregationalist minister, who took the boy (nicknamed "Ding" by his family) hunting and fishing. The young Darling's love of drawing followed him on these excursions. After receiving a degree from Beloit College in Wisconsin, Darling went to work at the *Des Moines Register* as a cartoonist. Soon, his cartoons were syndicated nationally by the *New York Tribune*, and collections of his cartoons began to be published in book form.

It was during this time that Darling began earning his reputation as "the best friend ducks ever had." His cartoons editorialized on the nation's attitude toward the outdoors; illegal hunting, hypocritical politicians, and the apathy of society were some of his favorite targets. One cartoon, titled "How Man Does Improve Upon Nature," shows two views of the same plot of land: one lush and tranquil, another rent by a muddy drainage ditch. In another, titled "Why Call Them Sportsmen?" a Mallard stands on crutches, his wing and foot broken, as he reads in a dictionary, "Sportsman: one who in sport is fair and generous." As he reads, the duck says, "Either this dictionary is wrong or there are a lot of folks around here calling themselves by the wrong name!"

In 1934, President Franklin Roosevelt appointed Darling chief of the U.S. Bureau of Biological Survey, the forerunner of today's Fish and Wildlife Service. There, Darling pushed for the enactment of the Migratory Bird Hunting Stamp Act, and when the bill became law, he designed the first federal duck stamp, *Mallards Dropping In*. Darling also chose the art for the next two duck stamps.

Darling's career spanned almost fifty years and garnered him two Pulitzer Prizes for journalism, a pair of honorary doctorates, and a host of public accolades. He died in February 1962, at the age of 85. Today, wildlife prospers at two lakes which bear his name: Lake Darling in Iowa and Lake Jay Darling in Saskatchewan, Canada.

Since 1937, the design for the federal duck stamp has been chosen through an annual competition. Until 1949, artist competition was by invitation only; in fact, the Bureau of Biological Survey asked only three artists to submit designs in the last year of invitation. In 1950, however, the contest was opened to all artists, unlocking

Federal 1934–35

Federal 1982–83

the floodgates to hundreds of artists every year, each of whom hopes he or she will submit the winning design. Currently, a new panel of five judges meets each year to evaluate the great volume of works submitted. In 1982, the judging panel eliminated 2,098 pieces of art before finally settling on David Maass' *Canvasbacks* as the winning entry.

The judging process begins as the panel spends several hours reviewing all the entries. The "first cut" is made when the entries which do not conform to printing specifications are eliminated from the contest. While artists are permitted to use any medium they wish for their entry (pen and ink, etching, pencil, watercolor, oil), all submissions must measure seven by ten inches and must be clear enough for the Bureau of Engraving and Printing to reproduce in miniature and in mass quantities.

Only those entries which have received favorable votes from at least three judges move into the next phase of the contest. The judges review the remaining designs once again and award each entry up to nine points. The highest and the lowest scores for each design are thrown out, and the five entries with the highest scores advance to the competition's final phase. Following another review by the judges, new scores are assigned and tallied, and the winning entry is selected.

Over the years, different trends have emerged in the design of the federal stamps. Early stamps, for instance, usually depicted scenes of birds in flight. A new dimension was added in 1970 when Edward Bierly's painting *Ross's Geese* was reproduced on the federal duck stamp in full color. The value of the addition of color to the series is fully realized by Bierly's print: originally sold for $60, at this writing a signed and numbered edition of the print with a mint-condition stamp is worth $2,700.

Changes in the rules have assured that two stamps will forever retain their unique standings in duck stamp collections. The 1959–60 design, *King Buck* by Maynard Reece, is a picture of a Labrador Retriever holding a Mallard. *Canvasback*, the 1975–76 design by James L. Fisher, features a Canvasback decoy in the foreground. Hunting themes have since been removed from the stamp designs, and today the rules state that stamp art cannot feature anything other than live waterfowl in their natural environment. As a result, the values of both *King Buck* and *Canvasback* have risen considerably.

Other rule changes have prohibited artists from depicting any species of duck which had appeared in the designs of the previous five years. Also, organizers of the program have attempted to infuse more action scenes into federal stamp art. For the 1986 and 1987 competition, judges were allowed to vote for any design they wished but were asked to concentrate on scenes depicting waterfowl in flight rather than sitting in the water.

The State Programs Begin

By the early 1970s, the federal program was an unqualified success. Millions had been raised for wetlands preservation, and roughly two and a half million stamps were being sold per year. However, California officials decided that they wanted their own method of raising funds for in-state conservation, independent of the federal government's control.

In 1971, California printed the nation's first state duck stamp, a monochromatic depiction of a pair of Pintails commissioned from artist Paul B. Johnson, which sold 178,245 stamps. Under the terms of his deal with the state, Johnson retained the publishing rights to the print. Five hundred prints were made, and the sales were brisk and encouraging.

Spurred by the success of the California program, Iowa became the second state to issue a duck stamp. For its first release, Iowa officials commissioned Maynard Reece. His design depicted three Mallards in flight. In 1974 two more states joined the ranks with duck stamp programs. The Maryland Department of Natural Resources commissioned John W. Taylor to create the design for that state's first stamp, and the Massachusetts Division of Fish and Wildlife commissioned Milton C. Weiler for the first stamp from that New England commonwealth. Weiler's design was a painting of a Wood Duck drake decoy carved by Joe Lincoln. All of Massachusetts' stamps to date have depicted decoys. In 1975, a Mallard in flight painted by artist Robert Eschenfeldt illustrated the Illinois first-of-state duck stamp.

These early state efforts were marked by trial and error. In California, Johnson continued his association with the fish and wildlife agency, creating designs for the state's first seven stamps. However, the partnership was marred by a clerical error, potentially costly to the artist, in the program's second year. Under the terms of the program, the stamps which were to accompany Johnson's prints were to be purchased by Johnson after the end of the hunting season, when the remaining nullified stamps were to be saved by the agency for six months and then shredded, thereby increasing the stamp's value among collectors. During the six months, Johnson was to be allowed to purchase 500 stamps at fifty percent of face value. However, instead of saving them, an agency clerk shredded the remaining stamps, forcing Johnson to collect as many stamps as he could through individual state offices. As a result, the 1972 California print edition consists of only 166 signed and numbered prints with matching stamps.

The death of Milton Weiler shortly after the release of the first Massachusetts Duck Stamp has caused confusion among dealers and collectors regarding the stamp's print edition. Following the stamp's release, a conservation group, Ducks Unlimited, produced a large, numbered, poster-type print of the stamp itself. Later, Weiler's heirs published 600 prints of the original decoy painting, the copyright of

California 1971

Iowa 1972

which was retained by the artist's family. Neither of the two print series was signed, but each Weiler family print was accompanied by a "Letter to the Owner," which was signed by the artist's son and correspondingly numbered to the print itself. Some collectors regard this print as being the true Massachusetts first-of-state print, while others argue that such a print must be signed and numbered by the artist himself to be authentic.

By 1976, duck stamps were such a successful fund raiser that four more states initiated programs: Indiana, Michigan, Mississippi, and South Carolina. Then 1977 and 1978 saw a brief decline in the number of new state programs; only two, in Minnesota and Wisconsin, released duck stamps in these years. But in 1979, five states entered the arena. Barbara Keel became the first woman to design a first-of-state stamp when her *Wood Ducks* was commissioned by the Alabama Department of Conservation. Florida and Missouri also commissioned artists for their first-of-state stamps in 1979, while Nevada and Tennessee each chose an artist through contests.

From 1980 to 1987, twenty-seven more states launched duck stamp programs. When Virginia selected a native artist, Ronald J. Louque, to create its first-of-state design in 1988, it became the forty-third state to sell duck stamps and prints to hunters and collectors. It is not only conceivable but probable that one day soon all fifty states will run duck stamp programs.

The states have used three methods to select designs for their first-of-state stamps: commissions, competitions, and bids. In commissioning works from major artists, states guarantee themselves and collectors a quality piece by an established artist, with a strong hope of hefty first-of-state sales revenues. But many states choose to open their programs to artists through design competitions; in fact, nearly three-quarters of the states with duck stamp programs accept competition entries annually. Contests in many states are open to artists from around the country, while some are restricted to state residents. Generally, states whose contests are nationwide have had the widest range of design styles from which to select, and these states have, for the most part, enjoyed higher sales margins.

Other states choose their designs by accepting bids for the jobs from publishers. In these instances, the entire operation is performed by the publisher, from the creation to the publication of the stamps and prints. By selecting from bids, states can not only judge the designs on their artistic merit, but also weigh which publisher will keep their costs lowest, affecting the amount they can raise for wetlands preservation. Ultimately, the latter is still the goal of any duck stamp program.

Federal and First-of-State Editions as Collectibles

Just as with postage stamp collecting, there are several ways in which duck stamps and prints can be collected.

The most common entry into a duck stamp collection is a single stamp in mint condition—that is, in its perfect, original state. "Non-mint" stamps, such as those bearing the signatures of hunting-license owners, are also collected but are not nearly as valuable.

Plate blocks are another form in which duck stamps are collected. These sets, consisting of four stamps taken from the corner of a sheet, are marked with the number of the plate with which they were printed. Finally, some collectors choose to collect the stamps by purchasing full sheets. Because the collector must pay the face value of each stamp in the sheet, the cost of purchasing full sheets makes this method of collecting less popular.

Today, prints are usually signed and numbered by the artist to ensure authenticity and increase value. A signed print with a number written on it guarantees that the print is part of an original, limited edition. Traditionally, artists number prints using two numerals separated by a slash mark. The first number is the number of the print, the second represents the size of the edition. Thus, a print numbered *235/500* is print number 235 in an edition totaling 500. Prints are not considered more or less valuable because they have a high or low print number.

Federal and first-of-state prints are commonly sold with accompanying mint-condition stamps. Over the years, however, artists, states, and publishers have found that other items commemorating the release of duck stamps are also popular with collectors.

Artist's and printer's proofs are prints that are inspected by artists and printers during the printing process. These prints are considered the cleanest, clearest reproductions of the original image. Artists number the prints they inspect, and these prints are considered more valuable, since they have been given the artist's personal approval. Printer's proofs are not numbered, but are still considered valuable. Maryland was the first to offer artist's proofs with its first-of-state print.

Remarques are original pieces of art, such as a painting or pencil drawing, which appear on the margin of the print itself. Remarqued prints are not only much more valuable than regular prints, but they also allow collectors to purchase an original piece of art at a fraction of the cost of a complete painting. Alabama, Florida, Missouri, Nevada, and Tennessee were the first states to include remarqued prints with their first-of-state releases. While both pencil and color remarques are common in state prints today, because of the size of the editions and the work involved in creating remarques, federal prints have not been remarqued since 1978.

To replace remarques in the federal releases, gold-plated medallions bearing likenesses of duck stamp designs were created in 1983. That year, Phil Scholer's print featuring a pair of Pintails was accompanied by a medallion commemorating the fiftieth federal issue. In the same year, Pennsylvania made medallions bearing the image of their first-of-state design, Ned Smith's *Sycamore Creek Woodies*. Today, the release of medallions is common among ongoing state programs.

The value of stamps and prints, based on many factors, is generally not agreed upon by all dealers and collectors. In fact, the dollar values mentioned in this introduction are based on insurance evaluations taken from estimated replacement costs. The value of federal and state duck stamps and prints can be determined by consulting several dealers and comparing the figures they cite.

As already stated, a stamp's condition is an important yardstick of its value. Stamps that are worn, creased, stained, frayed at the edges, or missing their glue backing have the least value. Mint stamps signed by the artist have the greatest value.

Besides the condition they are in, prints have many properties which determine value. The artist is sometimes the major factor to consider when speculating on the potential value of a new print. For instance, when the U.S. Fish and Wildlife Service selected Daniel Smith's design for the 1988–89 federal stamp, they chose an artist who had already won four first-of-state duck stamp competitions, as well as first-of-state turkey and pheasant stamp competitions and two other wildlife stamp contests. The 1988–89 federal stamp, therefore, would certainly seem to have a promising future for investors.

The number of prints in an edition—the edition size—also helps to determine a print's value. As with most collectibles, the rarer an item, the greater its worth, so prints with smaller edition sizes are generally worth more than prints with greater edition sizes. Most edition sizes are determined by the amount of orders received for a print by a specific date. This way, the size is determined directly by demand for the print at the time of its release. Because of its small edition size of 100 prints, the second federal print, a depiction of three Canvasbacks by Frank Weston Benson, is considered the rarest and most valuable in the entire duck stamp collection, and is worth approximately $7,000.

In some early releases, second and third editions of prints were made in order to satisfy public demand. Second and third editions are not as valuable as first editions, which can be as much as ten times more valuable than editions produced in later print runs.

Additionally, the value of stamps and prints can be established by the design of the art and the species depicted in it. Eye-catching pictures of species of waterfowl not seen in recent designs are usually the ones selected by federal and state governments and print publishers. Uniqueness in composition and subject is always a much-valued trait.

The Artists

If there is one group of men and women on whom the stamp programs depend for continued success, it is the artists who created the federal and first-of-state stamps on which this book is based. The life stories of most of the artists have common elements: an early and intense love of nature and wildlife, accompanied by artistic talent. Through the recognition associated with duck stamps and prints, several of these artists have reached the top of their profession.

Maynard Reece must be mentioned early in any discussion of America's best and most respected wildlife artists. In addition to his commission as artist for Iowa's first-of-state stamp (one of the most valuable first-of-state stamps in existence), Reece has won the federal competition a record five times, beginning in 1948. In all, he has designed twenty-two wildlife stamps, and over the years has committed himself to the goal of constantly improving his craft.

Another long-time artist but a relative newcomer to the world of duck stamps is Lee LeBlanc, who made an early mark through his association with one of the world's most famous aquatic fowls, Daffy Duck. An artist and animator for Warner Brothers' Merrie Melodies and Loony Tunes, LeBlanc entertained millions of movie-goers before he won the 1973–74 federal duck stamp competition with his painting, *Steller's Eiders*. In 1981, the same year his design won the contest for South Carolina's first-of-state stamp, he was commissioned to design Arkansas' initial release. LeBlanc also created the 1987 design for New York state.

Today, a younger generation of artists is taking its place alongside the pioneer duck stamp designers. In 1974, David Maass won his first federal design competition. Since then, he has created another federal stamp, two first-of-states, plus eight other stamp designs as his works have been commissioned by organizations dedicated to preserving a wide variety of wildlife, from ruffled grouse to wild turkeys.

Another wildlife artist to achieve prominence is Richard Plasschaert, who, between the years 1980 and 1983 alone, created a federal design and three first-of-state stamps. Plasschaert, a commercial artist skilled in a variety of media, also enjoys working on landscapes—noticeable in his design for the 1983 New Hampshire stamp—and portraits.

Born thirty years after the release of the first federal stamp, Tom Hirata created the first of his five duck stamp designs when he was chosen to do the first duck stamp for his home state of New Jersey in 1984. In the following three years, Hirata

• WATERFOWL STAMP •

$2.50   CANVASBACK

NEW JERSEY

VOID AFTER
JUNE 30, 1985

1984   047053

New Jersey 1984

was chosen four more times to design state duck stamps, including one from New Hampshire, one from Tennessee, and two consecutive stamps from North Carolina.

And that is just a sampling of the talent that has won praise across the country for beautiful renderings of America's waterfowl.

Results of the Duck Stamp Programs

The federal and first-of-state stamps not only represent the finest in American wildlife art, they reveal something of the national attitude toward the environment during the twentieth century. The emergence and subsequent success of the federal duck stamp program after continual environmental decay, and then of the many state programs launched in the 1970s and 1980s, are evidence of the American public's desire to regulate waterfowl hunting and to restrict mankind's encroachment upon virgin land.

The broad-scale attack upon American waterfowl had begun in the 1800s, and by the twentieth century hunters, unregulated and unrestrained, had decimated flocks all over the country. Millions of acres of wildlife habitats had been despoiled by a reckless development of roads, houses, and factories. Some species of waterfowl were in danger of extinction by the time the federal duck stamp program began in 1934.

Since then, the federal stamps alone have generated over $300 million, leading to the acquisition of more than three million acres of waterfowl habitats across the United States. Duck stamp funds have paid for all or part of more than 400 American wildlife refuges. The benefits of the stamp funds stretch far beyond ducks and geese, of course; the waterfowl habitats also serve as home for countless species of birds, mammals, fish, reptiles, and insects that make up the vital and fragile natural chain. Also, because of the refuges, naturalists are assured of a place to hike and bird-watch, and hunters can now pursue their pastime without endangering entire species of animals.

Duck stamps and prints are valuable and beautiful art objects that have earned their place alongside the books, dolls, glassware, postage stamps, coins, and other collectibles that have filled American homes and become part of people's lives. However, duck stamps and prints take on a special value when one considers that they also represent investments in our country's natural beauty.

American Waterfowl

1934–35 FEDERAL DUCK STAMP
Mallards Dropping In Jay Norwood Darling

The original art, a brush and ink design, measures 10″ × 14″. How the work was chosen is not known today.

The stamp is printed in blue ink and sold for $1.00. The first day of sale was August 14, 1934; 635,001 were sold.

The print was made by an etching process from a 5¾″ × 8½″ plate. The first edition probably numbers about 300. It was printed on white paper by Gordon Meaney from plates by René Lundgren. The first edition is not numbered, and it is unknown if there is a second edition.

1935–36 FEDERAL DUCK STAMP
Untitled (Canvasbacks)   **Frank Weston Benson**

The original art is a watercolor wash depicting Canvas-backs. It measures 5″ × 7″ and was chosen by the request of Jay N. Darling.

The stamp was printed in rose lake ink and sold for $1.00. The first day of sale was July 1, 1935. There were 448,204 sold.

The print was made by a hand-pulled etching process from a 3″ × 5″ plate. The first edition numbers 100, and was printed on light cream Shogun paper by John Peterson and Son Co. from plates by Frank Weston Benson. The first edition is not numbered. This print is the rarest and most valuable in the entire collection. There are believed to be imitations of this print that are slightly larger than the original.

16

1936–37   FEDERAL DUCK STAMP
Coming In   **Richard E. Bishop**

The original art is a drypoint etching of Canada Geese. It measures 9″ × 14⅞″ and was executed in 1931. It was chosen by the honorary request of Jay N. Darling.

The stamp was printed in black ink and sold for $1.00. The first day of sale was July 1, 1936; 603,623 were sold.

The print was made from a 5″ × 8″ plate created by the artist, who hand-pulled the prints on cream paper. To prevent wear from the printing process, Bishop used a chrome-faced plate. The prints are in an unnumbered edition.

1937–38 FEDERAL DUCK STAMP
Untitled (Greater Scaup) **Joseph D. Knap**

The original art, a watercolor wash in brown, depicting Greater Scaup in flight, measures 10½″ × 14½″. The work was chosen in an honorary limited competition.

The stamp was printed in light green ink and sold for $1.00. The first day of sale was July 1, 1937. There were 783,039 sold.

The print was made by fine-grained gravure from a 5¾″ × 8⅝″ plate and printed on off-white paper. There were 260 unnumbered first edition prints and there is probably not a second edition. The platemaker and printer are unknown. Above the image is the legend *Published and Copyrighted by the Sporting Gallery & Bookshop, Inc. Edition limited to 260 proofs.*

1938–39 FEDERAL DUCK STAMP
Untitled (Pintails) **Roland H. Clark**

The original art depicts five Pintails, but the plate was cut down and the artist's design altered, eliminating three birds. The work was chosen in an honorary limited competition.

The stamp was printed in light violet ink and sold for $1.00. The first day of sale was July 1, 1938; 1,002,715 were sold.

The print was made on off-white paper from a 6⅞″ × 11″ drypoint etching and the unnumbered first edition consists of about 300 prints. It is doubtful that a second edition was produced, and the design is out of print today. The printer is unknown; the plates were made by the artist.

1939–40 FEDERAL DUCK STAMP
Untitled (Green-Winged Teal) **Lynn Bogue Hunt, Sr.**

The original art, size unknown, depicts Green-Winged Teal.
The medium of the original art is graphite pencil. It was
chosen in an honorary limited competition.

The stamp was printed in chocolate brown and sold for $1.00.
The first day of sale was July 1, 1939; 1,111,561 were sold.

The print, measuring 7¾″ × 11″, is a stone lithograph, using
brownish black ink on white stock. The platemaker and printer
are unknown. The first edition is signed and numbered, but
the total is unknown. There is a second edition, quantity unknown, but prints marked *2nd E* are only a second state of
the first edition.

1940–41 FEDERAL DUCK STAMP
Untitled (Black Ducks) **Francis Lee Jaques**

The original art is a wash painting of two Black Ducks in flight. Its measurements are unknown. It was chosen in an honorary limited competition.

The stamp was printed in sepia and sold for $1.00. The first day of sale was July 1, 1940; 1,260,810 were sold.

The print is a stone lithograph; the actual image of the vignette is about 7¼″ × 10″ with the matted area about 9½″ × 12½″. The black ink is printed on white, probably Curtis, stock. The first and second edition stones were made by the artist and the third edition stone by Ellison Hoover, artist and cartoonist. The three editions totaled around 260 prints. The prints are not numbered, but they are signed.

1941–42 FEDERAL DUCK STAMP
Ruddy Ducks   Edwin Richard Kalmbach

The original art is a wash with some gouache details, but its size is unknown. It was chosen in an honorary limited competition.

The stamp was printed in brown carmine and sold for $1.00. The first day of sale was July 1, 1941; 1,439,967 were sold.

The print in its second edition was handled by the artist. The medium of this 7″ × 9″ print is possibly fine-grain gravure, using black ink on white stock. The platemaker and printer was Bradford-Robinson Printing Co. The quantity of both editions is unknown. The first edition print, titled *Migratory Bird Hunting Stamp, 1941–42* and signed E. R. Kalmbach, was flopped left to right. It is believed to measure about 6½″ × 8¾″ in an edition of possibly 100 to 110 (unconfirmed), and was printed by Geo. C. Miller & Son, Inc.

1942–43   FEDERAL DUCK STAMP
American Widgeon   **Alden Lassell Ripley**

The original art, size unknown, is a sketch in pencil and pen of Widgeon in the water and landing. It was chosen in an honorary limited competition.

The stamp was printed in brown and sold for $1.00. The first day of sale was July 1, 1942; 1,383,629 were sold.

The print, measuring 6″ × 8½″, is a drypoint etching, using warm black ink on white stock. The artist made the plates, and the printer was John Peterson & Son Company. The quantity of the first edition is unknown. It is signed A. Lassell Ripley. This *artist's original print* is both aesthetically and technically a fine example of drypoint.

1943–44 FEDERAL DUCK STAMP
Untitled (Wood Ducks) **Walter E. Bohl**

The original art is a 5″ (shy) × 7″ drypoint etching on copper of Wood Ducks in flight. It was chosen in an honorary limited competition.

The stamp was printed in Indian red and sold for $1.00. The first day of sale was July 1, 1943; 1,169,352 were sold.

The print, measuring 5″ (shy) × 7″ is a drypoint etching on copper, using black ink on white Rives stock. The first edition numbers 290 and is signed Walter E. Bohl. The second edition is in two states: the first state is not labelled; the second state is labelled *II*. Since the artist made the plate·and did the printing, this is an *artist's original print*. The first edition can be identified by the measurement from the upper wing to top plate mark, a scant ⅛″; in the second edition, the same measurement is ¼″.

1944–45 FEDERAL DUCK STAMP
White-Fronted Geese **Walter A. Weber**

The original art is a 5″ × 7″ wash showing the birds in flight. It was chosen in an honorary limited competition.

The stamp was printed in orange and sold for $1.00. The first day of sale was July 1, 1944; 1,487,029 were sold.

The print is a stone lithograph; the vignette at the bottom has an actual image of 6½″ × 9½″. It was printed with black and sepia inks on white Rives Heavy stock. The platemaker is unknown; the printer was Geo. C. Miller & Son, Inc. The first edition consists of 100 flopped prints that are unnumbered but signed Walter A. Weber. The second edition comprises 200 right reading prints, and the third edition comprises 90 numbered and signed black and white stone lithographs with greenish-gray background tint block, with stone drawn by Mr. Weber and printing by Geo. C. Miller & Son, Inc. This is an *original print* but not an *artist's original*, another artist having done the drawing on the stone.

1945–46 FEDERAL DUCK STAMP
Shovelers **Owen J. Gromme**

The original art is a 5″ × 7″ wash showing Shovelers in flight. It was chosen in an honorary limited competition.

The stamp was printed in black and white and sold for $1.00. The first day of sale was July 1, 1945; 1,725,505 were sold.

The print is a 5″ × 7″ fine-grain gravure, using black ink on white stock. The platemaker is unknown and the printer was possibly Beck Engraving Company. The first edition is 250. They are signed Owen J. Gromme. This is a *printer's print* since it was transferred photographically, and it bears the legend *Copyright 1945 by the F. H. Bresler Co., Milwaukee,* in script type over the image at the left. The print is very difficult to obtain today.

1946–47 FEDERAL DUCK STAMP
Redheads Robert W. Hines

The original art, size and medium unknown, was chosen in an honorary limited competition.

The stamp was printed in brown and black and sold for $1.00. The first day of sale was July 1, 1946; 2,016,841 were sold.

The print is an 8⅛″ × 11″ stone lithograph, printed with black ink on white stock. The platemaker was the artist and the printer is unknown. The quantity of the first edition is unknown, possibly 300. It was signed Bob Hines 1946; it is not known if it is numbered. There is a second edition of 385. This *artist's original print* is notated *B-31* in pencil.

1947–48 FEDERAL DUCK STAMP
From Beyond the North Wind **Jack Murray**

The original art is 14″ × 18½″ in what appears to be wash and gouache. It shows two Snow Geese in flight. It was chosen in an honorary limited competition.

The stamp was printed in black and sold for $1.00. The first day of sale was July 1, 1947; 1,722,677 were sold.

The print is an 8⅛″ × 11⅜″ fine-grain gravure, black ink on off-white stock. The platemaker and printer was Thomas J. Foley. The first edition is 300, unnumbered, and signed Jack Murray © 1947. This is a *printer's print* since it was photographically transferred.

1948–49 FEDERAL DUCK STAMP
Buffleheads Aloft   **Maynard Reece**

The original art is a 5″ × 7″ wash and gouache painting of the birds in flight. It was chosen in an honorary invitational competition with some freely submitted designs.

The stamp was printed in brilliant light blue and sold for $1.00. The first day of sale was July 1, 1948; 2,127,603 were sold.

The print is a 6¾″ × 9⅛″ stone lithograph, black ink on white Rives Heavy stock. The platemaker for the first edition was C. W. Anderson; for the second edition it was the artist. The printer was Geo. C. Miller & Son, Inc. The first edition is 200 prints; they are unnumbered and signed Maynard Reece. There is a second edition of 150 plus 25 artist's proofs, a third edition of 400, and a fourth edition of 350. This is an *artist's original print* since Mr. Reece did the drawing on the two stones. The fourth edition was printed in full color using offset lithography.

1949–50 FEDERAL DUCK STAMP
American Goldeneyes Roger E. Preuss

The original art is a 5″ × 7″ wash of the birds in flight and in the water. It was chosen in honorary invitational competition supplemented by some freely submitted designs.

The stamp was printed in brilliant green and sold for $2.00. The first day of sale was July 1, 1949; 1,954,734 were sold.

The print is a 6⅝″ × 9⅛″ stone lithograph, black ink on white Rives Heavy stock. The platemaker was C. W. Anderson and the printer was Geo. C. Miller & Son, Inc. The first edition is 250 unnumbered prints, signed Rog [or Roger] E. Preuss. Some bear the date 1949. The artist remarqued in pencil eight of the prints from the edition.

1950–51 FEDERAL DUCK STAMP
Trumpeter Swans **Walter A. Weber**

The original art is a 5″ × 7″ wash and gouache painting of the birds in flight. It was chosen in open national competition (this was the first open national competition). The design was chosen from 88 designs by 65 artists.

The stamp was printed in brilliant bluish purple and sold for $2.00. The first day of sale was July 1, 1950; 1,903,644 were sold.

The print is a 5″ × 7″ fine-grain gravure, blue-gray ink on white stock. The platemaker and printer was Beck Engraving Company. For the first edition 500 were made, about 250 (possibly fewer) signed, and the balance lost. It is signed Walter A. Weber. There is a second edition of 300 numbered and signed 7″ × 10⅛″ prints. This is a *printer's print*, transferred photographically. *Copyright 1950 Walter A. Weber* appears in the margin at the upper left.

1951–52 FEDERAL DUCK STAMP
Gadwalls **Maynard Reece**

The original art is a 5″ × 7″ wash and gouache painting of Gadwalls taking off. It was chosen in open national competition from 74 designs by 51 artists.

The stamp was printed in dark or smoke gray and sold for $2.00. The first day of sale was July 1, 1951; 2,167,767 were sold.

The print is a 6¾″ × 9⅛″ stone lithograph, black ink on white Rives Heavy stock. The platemaker was the artist and the printer was Geo. C. Miller & Son, Inc. The first edition comprises 250 unnumbered prints, signed Maynard Reece. There is a second edition of 400. This is an *artist's original print* since Mr. Reece made the drawing on the stone. The second edition carries the notation *2nd ed.*

1952–53 FEDERAL DUCK STAMP
Untitled (Harlequins) **John Henry Dick**

The original art is a 5″ × 7″ wash of Harlequins in flight. It was chosen in open national competition from an unknown number of entries.

The stamp was printed in a reduced red shade of blue, or lilac blue, and sold for $2.00. The first day of sale was July 1, 1952; 2,296,628 were sold.

The print is a 7⅛″ × 9⅜″ stone lithograph, black ink on white Curtis stock. The platemaker was possibly C. W. Anderson and the printer was Geo. C. Miller & Son, Inc. The quantity of the first edition is not known (possibly 250). It is unnumbered and is signed John H. Dick. There is a second edition of 300. This is an *original print* but not an artist's original because the drawing on the stone was done by another artist.

1953–54 FEDERAL DUCK STAMP
Early Express   **Clayton B. Seagears**

The original art is a 5″ × 7″ India ink wash drawing of Blue-Winged Teal in flight. It was chosen in open national competition from 92 entries by 53 artists.

The stamp was printed in maroon and sold for $2.00. The first day of sale was July 1, 1953; 2,268,446 were sold.

The print is a 6¾″ × 9″ stone lithograph, black ink on white stock. The platemaker was C. W. Anderson and the printer was Geo. C. Miller & Son, Inc. The quantity of the first edition is possibly 250. It is signed Clayt Seagears. The second edition, using offset lithography, is 1500.

1954–55 FEDERAL DUCK STAMP
Ring-Necks **Harvey Dean Sandstrom**

The original art is a 5″ × 7″ gouache drawing of the birds in flight. It was chosen in open national competition from 114 entries by 87 artists.

The stamp was printed in black and white and sold for $2.00. The first day of sale was July 1, 1954; 2,184,550 were sold.

The print is a 5″ × 7″ stone lithograph, black ink on white stock. The platemaker was C. W. Anderson and the printer was Geo. C. Miller & Son, Inc. The first edition comprises 250 unnumbered prints, signed Harvey D. Sandstrom. There is a second edition of 400. The high quality of the print is maintained through both editions.

1955–56   FEDERAL DUCK STAMP
Blue Geese   **Stanley Stearns**

The original art is a 5″ × 7″ ink and pencil drawing on scratch-board of Blue Geese in flight. It was chosen in open national competition from 93 designs by 66 artists.

The stamp was printed in a warm, medium dark blue and sold for $2.00. The first day of sale was July 1, 1955; 2,369,940 were sold.

The print is a 7½″ × 10½″ etching and aquatint on a chrome-faced copper plate made by the artist. The first edition comprises 250 unnumbered signed prints from two printings. The first is in warm black ink. The second is in brown ink and carries the mark *ST*.

1956–57 FEDERAL DUCK STAMP
American Mergansers **Edward J. Bierly**

The original art is a 5″ × 7″ gouache drawing showing the birds in flight. It was chosen in open national competition from 64 designs by 42 artists.

The stamp was printed in blue-black and sold for $2.00. The first day of sale was July 1, 1956; 2,332,014 were sold.

The print is a 5″ × 7″ etching and aquatint, steel-faced, using black ink on ivory finish Rives for the first printing and white Linweave stock for the second. The platemaker was the artist and the printer was Andersen-Lamb Photogravure Corporation. The first edition comprises 450 unnumbered signed prints.

1957–58 FEDERAL DUCK STAMP
American Eiders **Jackson Miles Abbott**

The original art is a 5″ × 7″ gouache drawing of the birds in flight. It was chosen in open national competition from 106 entries by 60 artists.

The stamp was printed in a medium yellowish green and sold for $2.00. The first day of sale was July 1, 1957; 2,355,353 were sold.

The print is a 7½″ × 9¾″ stone lithograph, black ink on white stock. The platemaker was C. W. Anderson and the printer was Geo. C. Miller & Son, Inc. The first edition comprises 250 unnumbered prints, signed Jackson M. Abbott. There is a second edition of 500 and a third of 1500. The third edition was printed by four-color offset lithography.

1958–59 FEDERAL DUCK STAMP
Canada Geese   Leslie C. Kouba

The original art is a 5″ × 7″ wash of the birds landing and on the ground. It was chosen in open national competition over 96 entries by 55 artists.

The stamp was printed in midnight black and sold for $2.00. The first day of sale was July 1, 1958; 2,176,425 were sold.

The print is a 6 ⅞″ × 9 ¼″ stone lithograph for the first edition; the second edition is a 7″ × 9″ drypoint etching and aquatint. The ink is black on white stock in the first edition and black on off-white Early American stock in the second edition. The platemaker for the first edition was C.W. Anderson and for the second edition was the artist. The printer for the first edition was Geo. C. Miller & Son, Inc., and for the second edition, Cornelis A. Bartels. The first edition comprises 250 unnumbered prints entitled *Federal Duck Stamp Design, 1958–59* and signed Les C. Kouba. The second edition numbers 250, and a third edition, in four-color offset lithography, numbers 300.

1959–60 FEDERAL DUCK STAMP
King Buck **Maynard Reece**

The original art is a 5″ × 7″ wash and gouache painting of a Labrador Retriever, King Buck, retrieving a Mallard. It was chosen in open national competition from 110 entries by 64 artists.

The stamp was printed in black, blue, and yellow and sold for $3.00. The first day of sale was July 1, 1959; 1,626,115 were sold.

The print, a best-seller, is a 6⅝″ × 9⅛″ stone lithograph, black ink on white Rives Heavy stock. The platemaker was the artist, and the printer was Geo. C. Miller & Son, Inc. The first edition comprises 400 unnumbered signed prints. There is a second edition of 300 and a third of 400.

1960–61 FEDERAL DUCK STAMP
Redhead Ducks   John A. Ruthven

The original art is a 5″ × 7″ gouache drawing of Redheads in water. It was chosen in open national competition over an unknown number of entries.

The stamp was printed in yellow, crimson-brown, and bonnie blue and sold for $3.00. The first day of sale was July 1, 1960; 1,725,634 were sold.

The print, 6¾″ × 9¼″, was hand-painted on grained zinc plate (lithograph), using black ink on off-white stock. The platemaker was the artist and the printer was Strobridge Litho Company. The first edition comprises 400 unnumbered signed prints. The second edition numbers 400. There is a third edition of 450 hand-colored drypoint etchings.

1961–62 FEDERAL DUCK STAMP
Nine Mallards **Edward A. Morris**

The original art is a 5″ × 7″ wash of a family of Mallards in water. It was chosen in open national competition from 100 entries from an unknown number of artists.

The stamp was printed in red-brown, yellow-brown, and light blue and sold for $3.00. The first day of sale was July 1, 1961; 1,344,236 were sold.

The print is a 6⅝″ × 5¼″ drypoint etching and aquatint, using black ink on antique white English Text stock. The platemaker and the printer was Cornelis A. Bartels. The first edition comprises 250 unnumbered prints, signed Edward A. Morris.

1962–63 FEDERAL DUCK STAMP
Pintails Edward A. Morris

The original art is a 5″ × 7″ wash of the birds landing. It was chosen in open national competition from an unknown number of entries.

The stamp was printed in black, purple-blue, and red-brown and sold for $3.00. The first day of sale was July 1, 1962; 1,147,212 were sold.

The print is a 6½″ × 9″ drypoint etching and aquatint, using black ink on antique white English Text stock. The platemaker and printer was Cornelis A. Bartels. The first edition comprises 250 unnumbered signed prints. This is the only time an artist has won the federal competition twice in a row.

1963–64 FEDERAL DUCK STAMP
American Brant   **Edward J. Bierly**

The original art is a 5″ × 7″ gouache of the birds about to land. It was chosen in open national competition from 161 designs by 87 artists.

The stamp was printed in pale blue, orange-yellow, and black and sold for $3.00. The first day of sale was July 1, 1963; 1,448,191 were sold.

The print is a 7″ × 9″ etching and aquatint, steel faced, using warm black ink on white Rives stock for the first printing and white Linweave stock for the second. The platemaker was the artist and the printer was Andersen-Lamb Photogravure Corp. The first edition comprises 675 unnumbered signed prints. There are two printings, one of 550 and a second of 125.

44

1964–65 FEDERAL DUCK STAMP
Nene High Among the Lava Flows   **Stanley Stearns**

The original art is a 5″ × 7″ wash and gouache drawing of Nene Geese. It was chosen in open national competition from 158 entries by 87 artists.

The stamp was printed in blue, khaki, yellow, and black and sold for $3.00. The first day of sale was July 1, 1964; 1,573,155 were sold.

The print is a 7½″ × 10½″ stone lithograph, black ink on white Rives Heavy stock. The platemaker was the artist and the printer was Geo. C. Miller & Son, Inc. The first edition comprises 665 unnumbered signed prints. There is a second edition of 100. Second edition prints have *II © 1964 ST* in the lower right and carry *2nd ed.* and the number in pencil. Ten of these are hand-colored, numbered 1 through 10, and labelled.

1965–66 FEDERAL DUCK STAMP
Canvasbacks Ron Jenkins

The original art is a 5″ × 7″ gouache (with photo-retouch grays) of the birds in flight. It was chosen in open national competition from 138 entries by 85 artists.

The stamp was printed in two browns and two greens and sold for $3.00. The first day of sale was July 1, 1965; 1,558,197 were sold.

The print is a 5¼″ × 9½″ stone lithograph, black ink on white Rives Heavy stock. The platemaker was the artist and the printer was Geo. C. Miller & Son, Inc. The first edition comprises 700 unnumbered signed prints. Numbers 1 through 9 were hand-colored by the artist. There are two printings of the first edition—500 and 200; they are indistinguishable. A second edition of 100 was done by offset on Linweave 125-lb. white stock; it is labelled *Canvasbacks II*, printed by Delaneys. Ten of these were hand-colored by the artist, numbered 1 through 10, and labelled. There is a third edition of 250 block prints on 65-lb. Gray Rippletone Hammermill Cover stock.

1966–67 FEDERAL DUCK STAMP
Whistling Swans   **Stanley Stearns**

The original art is a 5″ × 7″ wash and gouache (polymer) drawing of the birds in flight over the water. It was chosen from 181 designs by 105 artists.

The stamp was printed in black, blue, and green and sold for $3.00. The first day of sale was July 1, 1966; 1,805,341 were sold.

The print is a 7½″ × 10½″ stone lithograph, black ink on white Rives Heavy stock. The platemaker was the artist and the printer was Geo. C. Miller & Son, Inc. The first edition comprises 300 numbered, unsigned prints. There is a second edition of 300. First edition prints have © *ST 1966* in the lower right corner of the print. Second edition prints, in addition to being labelled so in pencil, have *II © 1966* in the lower right corner of the print. Ten of these are hand-colored, numbered 1 through 10, and labelled.

1967–68 FEDERAL DUCK STAMP
Old Squaw—Tree River, N.W.T. **Leslie C. Kouba**

The original art is a 5″ × 7″ wash and gouache drawing of the birds on the ground. It was chosen in open national competition from 170 entries.

The stamp was printed in blue, brown, and yellow and sold for $3.00. The first day of sale was July 1, 1967; 1,934,697 were sold.

The print is a 6¾″ × 9¼″ drypoint and aquatint, using black ink on antique white English Text stock. The platemaker and the printer was Cornelis A. Bartels. The first edition comprises 250 (to date) unnumbered signed prints. Changes were made to the sky during printing, so there are two states of this print: 100 first state prints and 150 second state prints.

1968–69   FEDERAL DUCK STAMP
Poised   **Claremont Gale Pritchard**

The original art is a 5″ × 7″ wash of Hooded Mergansers at rest. There are two copies: (1) a 7″ × 11″ pastel and (2) a large painting in Pioneer Village, Minden, Nebraska. It was chosen in open national competition from 184 entries.

The stamp was printed in black, brown, and green and sold for $3.00. The first day of sale was July 1, 1968; 1,837,139 were sold.

The print is a 6⅝″ × 9¼″ stone lithograph, black ink on white Rives Heavy stock. The platemaker was Stanley Malzman and the printer was Geo. C. Miller & Son, Inc. The first edition comprises 750 numbered prints.

1969–70   FEDERAL DUCK STAMP
White-Winged Scoters   **Maynard Reece**

The original art is a 5″ × 7″ wash of the birds taking off. It was chosen in open national competition from 218 entries.

The stamp was printed in red, brown, slate blue, and black and sold for $3.00. The first day of sale was July 1, 1969; 2,072,108 were sold.

The print is a 6½″ × 9¼″ stone lithograph, black ink on white Rives Heavy stock. The platemaker was the artist and the printer was Geo. C. Miller & Son, Inc. The first edition comprises 750 numbered prints.

1970–71 FEDERAL DUCK STAMP
Ross's Geese **Edward J. Bierly**

The original art is a 5″ × 7″ watercolor of the birds in the water. It was chosen in open national competition from 148 entries.

The stamp was printed in yellow-red, blue, green, and black and sold for $3.00. The first day of sale was July 1, 1970; 2,420,244 were sold.

The print is a 7″ × 9¾″ four-color photolithograph, using unknown inks with special fade-resistant coating on white Weyerhauser 80-lb. Carousel Cover stock. The separation negative maker and the printer was Edmund A. Loper. The first edition comprises 300 remarqued prints (numbered 1–300) and 700 regular prints (numbered 1–700). There is only one printing of the first edition, and it is not known if the separation negatives were destroyed. There is a second edition of 2150. This is the first year the print was in full color.

1971–72 FEDERAL DUCK STAMP
Cinnamon Teal **Maynard Reece**

The original art is a 5″ × 7″ full-color wash of the birds coming in to land. It was chosen in open national competition from 191 entries.

The stamp was printed in full color and sold for $3.00. The first day of sale was July 1, 1971; 2,445,977 were sold.

The print is a 6⅝″ × 9¼″ stone lithograph, hand-pulled, printed with black and tan inks on white Rives Heavy stock. The platemaker was the artist and the printer was Geo. C. Miller & Son, Inc. The first edition comprises 950 numbered prints. Each print carries the initials of the person who hand-colored it: JR for June Reece, MAR for Mark Reece, and BR for Brad Reece.

1971 FIRST CALIFORNIA DUCK STAMP
Pintails **Paul B. Johnson**

The original art depicts a pair of Pintails in flight. Mr. Johnson was commissioned by the California Department of Fish and Game to design the artwork for the first state waterfowl stamp.

The stamp is numbered on the front. It sold for $1.00. Of the 400,000 stamps that were printed, 178,245 were sold.

The print is 5¾″ × 7½″. The edition consists of 500 signed and numbered and 150 Executive Series prints.

1972–73   FEDERAL DUCK STAMP
Emperor Geese   **Arthur M. Cook**

The original art is a 5″ × 7″ watercolor of the birds about to
land. It was chosen in open national competition from 213
entries.

The stamp was printed in full color and sold for $5.00. The
first day of sale was July 1, 1972; 2,184,343 were sold.

The print is a 6⅜″ × 9″ photolithograph (five-color process),
using an unknown ink on white Strathmore Beau Brilliant
stock. The separation negative maker and the printer was R.R.
Donnelly & Sons, Inc. The first edition comprises 950 numbered prints. The remarqued prints are numbered 1 through
200; the regular prints, 201 through 950. The first 200 are
remarqued. There is a second edition of 900, of which 100
have remarques in color and 300 in pencil.

1972   FIRST IOWA DUCK STAMP
Mallards   **Maynard Reece**

The original art depicts three Mallards in flight. Mr. Reece, a renowned wildlife artist, was commissioned by the Iowa Conservation Commission to design the artwork for the initial Iowa waterfowl stamp.

The stamp is not numbered. It sold for $1.00. Of the 125,000 stamps that were printed, 70,446 were sold. The remainders were sold until June 1978.

The print is 6⁷⁄₁₆″ × 11″. The edition consists of 500 signed and numbered prints.

1973–74 FEDERAL DUCK STAMP
Steller's Eiders **Lee LeBlanc**

The original art is a 5″ × 7″ opaque watercolor painting of
the birds at rest. It was chosen in open national competition
from 249 entries.

The stamp was printed in full color and sold for $5.00. The
first day of sale was July 1, 1973; 2,094,414 were sold.

The print is a 6½″ × 9″ four-color photolithograph, using
Sleight-Hellmuth inks on 100-lb. Curtis Stoneridge Menu Cover
stock. The separation negative maker was Colorcraft, Inc., and
the printer was NAPCO Graphic Arts, Inc. The first edition
comprises 1000 numbered prints. There is a second edition
of 600 signed and numbered prints and 300 remarqued.

1974–75 FEDERAL DUCK STAMP
Wood Ducks **David A. Maass**

The original art is a 5″ × 7″ oil painting; a larger oil painting was done for the print. It was chosen in open national competition from 291 entries.

The stamp was printed in full color and sold for $5.00. The first day of sale was July 1, 1974; 2,214,056 were sold.

The print is a 6½″ × 9″ four-color photolithograph, using specially compounded lite-fast inks on 100-lb. Warrens Lustro Dull, Saxony Finish Cover stock. The separation negative maker and the printer was Johnson Printing, Inc. The first edition was not limited to a specific number, and the prints are unnumbered.

1974 FIRST MARYLAND DUCK STAMP
Mallards **John W. Taylor**

The original art depicts a pair of Mallards in the snow. Mr. Taylor was commissioned by the Maryland Department of Natural Resources to design this first Maryland State Waterfowl Stamp.

The stamp is numbered on an attached tab. It sold for $1.10. All 90,000 stamps that were printed were sold.

The print is 6⅜" × 9". The edition consists of 500 signed and numbered prints plus artist's proofs.

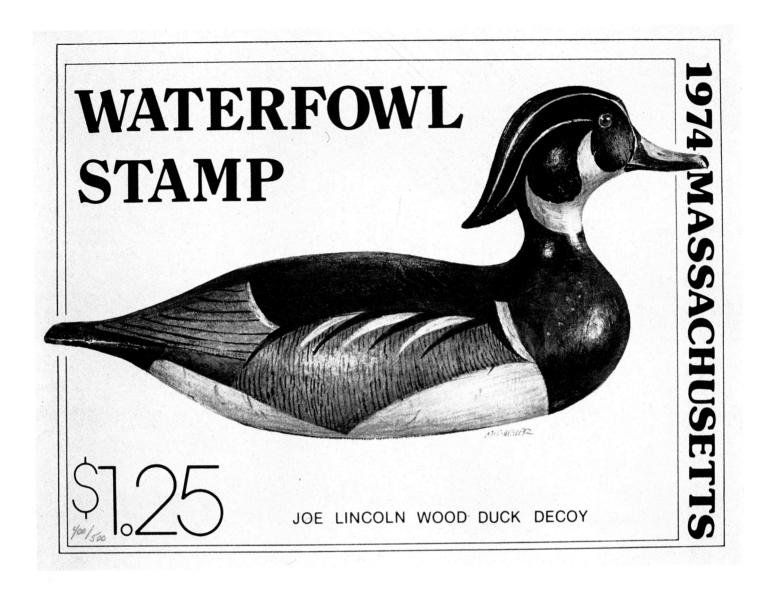

$1.25

JOE LINCOLN WOOD DUCK DECOY

1974   FIRST MASSACHUSETTS DUCK STAMP
Wood Duck Decoy   **Milton C. Weiler**

The original art was commissioned from Mr. Weiler by the Massachusetts Division of Fisheries and Wildlife. It was the state's first waterfowl stamp. The design features a Wood Duck drake decoy carved by Joe Lincoln.

The stamp is not numbered. It sold for $1.25. All of the 50,400 stamps that were printed were sold.

The print size of 7″ × 9″ refers to the later print published by Mr. Weiler's heirs. That edition consists of 600 prints. There is also a larger print published by Ducks Unlimited that is a reproduction of the stamp itself. Neither of the editions is signed by the artist because of Mr. Weiler's death in 1974.

1975—76   FEDERAL DUCK STAMP
Canvasback   **James P. Fisher**

The original art is a 5″ × 7″ watercolor of a Canvasback decoy. It was chosen in open national competition from 268 entries.

The stamp was printed in full color and sold for $5.00. The first day of sale was July 1, 1975; 2,237,126 were sold.

The print is 6½″ × 9″, a combination of offset lithograph and collotype (using seven colors). The stock is Arches 88 (100% rag content), and the separation negative maker and the printer was Triton Press, Inc. The first edition numbers 3150, and the prints are numbered and untitled. This is the first and only federal design to feature a decoy. The contest rules have been revised and now read that, beginning with the 1976–77 stamp, the principal subject of the duck stamp entries must be living waterfowl.

1975 FIRST ILLINOIS DUCK STAMP
Mallard   **Robert Eschenfeldt**

The original art depicts a Mallard drake in flight. The Illinois Department of Conservation commissioned the artist to design the first state waterfowl stamp.

The stamp is numbered on the front. It sold for $5.25. Of the 200,000 stamps that were printed, 60,377 were sold. All remainders were destroyed on June 30, 1982.

The print is 7″ × 9″. The edition consists of 500 signed and numbered prints.

1976–77 FEDERAL DUCK STAMP
Canada Geese **Alderson Magee**

The original art is a 5″ × 7″ scratchboard rendering of Canada Geese in the water. There is one copy at a 6½″ × 9″ size. It was chosen in open national competition from 264 entries.

The stamp was printed in black and light green and sold for $5.00. The first day of sale was July 1, 1976; 2,170,194 were sold.

The print is a 6½″ × 9″ photolithograph in a three-plate process, using special lite-fast inks. The stock is Triton 100-lb. cover, neutral pH. The separation negative maker and the printer was Triton Press, Inc. The first edition consists of 3600 signed and numbered prints and 1000 with companion pieces. It is important to note that although the print appears to be in black and white, the softness and dimension achieved were possible only because the print was actually printed in three colors, warm black, cool black, and sepia—an excellent example of superior printing techniques.

MIGRATORY BIRD HUNTING STAMP

VOID AFTER JUNE 30, 1977

$5

CANADA-GEESE

U.S. DEPARTMENT OF THE INTERIOR

1976 FIRST INDIANA DUCK STAMP
Green-Winged Teal **Justus H. ("Sonny") Bashore**

The original art depicts a Green-Winged Teal drake in flight. The Indiana Department of Natural Resources commissioned the artist to design the artwork for the state's first waterfowl stamp.

The stamp is numbered on the front. It sold for $5.00. There were 70,000 stamps printed.

The print is 6″ × 9″. The edition consists of 500 signed and numbered prints. This is the only stamp print in the Indiana series that was offered for sale nationally. All reproduction rights regarding sales of prints after 1976 were retained by the Department of Natural Resources, according to the rules of the contest.

1976 FIRST MICHIGAN DUCK STAMP
Wood Duck   Oscar Warbach

The original art depicts a Wood Duck drake. The Michigan Department of Natural Resources commissioned the artist to design the artwork for Michigan's initial duck stamp.

The stamp is numbered on the front. It sold for $2.10. Of the 250,000 stamps that were printed, 92,802 were sold. The remainders were disposed of in July 1978.

The print is $4^{11}/_{16}'' \times 8''$. The edition consists of 500 signed and numbered prints.

1976   FIRST MISSISSIPPI DUCK STAMP
Wood Duck   Carroll J. and Gwen K. Perkins

The original art for the first Mississippi waterfowl stamp is a photograph of a Wood Duck swimming in calm water. It was taken from a blind on the shore of a small pond. The artists were commissioned to design this initial stamp by the Mississippi Game and Fish Commission.

The stamp is numbered on the front. It sold for $2.00. There were 50,000 stamps printed.

The print is 6½″ × 9⅜″. The edition consists of 500 signed and numbered prints.

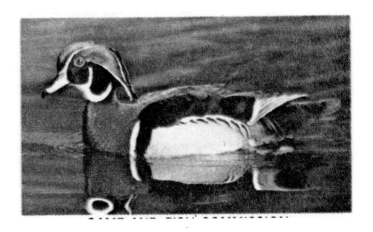

1976 FIRST SOUTH DAKOTA DUCK STAMP
Mallards **Robert Kusserow**

The original art depicts a pair of Mallards, one in the water and one coming in for a landing. This was the first waterfowl stamp contest for South Dakota. (Only residents of South Dakota are eligible to enter the contest.)

The stamp is numbered on the front. It sold for $1.00. Of the 89,000 stamps that were printed, 38,788 were sold.

The print is 6½″ × 9″. The edition consists of 500 signed and numbered prints. Matching numbered stamps were offered with each print in the edition for the first time.

1977–78   FEDERAL DUCK STAMP
Ross's Geese   **Martin R. Murk**

The original art is a 5″ × 7″ acrylic rendering of Ross's Geese in flight. It was chosen in open national competition from 264 entries.

The stamp was printed in full color and sold for $5.00. The first day of sale was July 1, 1977; 2,196,774 were sold.

The print is a 6 ½″ × 9″ photolithograph in six colors, using permanent, lite-fast inks. The stock is Gallery 100 plate finish (100% rag), and the separation negative maker and printer was Wetzel Brothers, Inc. The first edition consists of 5800 numbered prints. The image's subtlety was enhanced by the addition of a fifth and sixth color in printing.

1977 FIRST MINNESOTA DUCK STAMP
Mallards   David A. Maass

The original art depicts three Mallards taking flight. The Minnesota Department of Natural Resources commissioned the artist to design the artwork for the first state waterfowl stamp and print. This design is the official logo of the Minnesota Waterfowl Association; the department selected it in recognition of the efforts of the Waterfowl Association.

The stamp is numbered on the back. It sold for $3.50. There were 300,000 stamps printed.

The print is 6½″ × 9″. This was a time-limited edition taken to order. The quantity has never been officially published, but it is believed to be approximately 3300 signed but unnumbered prints. This print marks the turning point in the expansion of print sales of state duck stamp prints, being the first edition size to number over 500 on a first-of-state issue.

1978–79 FEDERAL DUCK STAMP
Hooded Merganser **Albert Earl Gilbert**

The original art is a 5″ × 7″ opaque watercolor. It was chosen in open national competition from 296 entries.

The stamp was printed in full color and sold for $5.00. The first day of sale was July 1, 1978; 2,206,421 were sold.

The print is a 7″ × 9⅞″ photolithograph in six colors, using lite-fast inks. The stock is 100% rag Mont-Lith Vellum 140 lb., and the separation negative maker and printer was Litho-Craft of New England. The first edition is 5800 regular plus 1350 remarqued. The edition is numbered and is the first federal print to have watercolor remarques. This means the artist had to consider three things when selecting the paper: it had to be acid free, it had to accept ink well, and it had to receive a watercolor remarque without buckling or repelling the paint.

69

1978   FIRST WISCONSIN DUCK STAMP
Wood Ducks   Owen J. Gromme

The original art depicts three Wood Ducks in flight. The Wisconsin Department of Natural Resources commissioned Mr. Gromme to design the artwork for this initial state waterfowl stamp.

The stamp is numbered on an attached tab. It sold for $3.25. All of the 280,000 stamps that were printed were sold.

The print is 6½″ × 9″. The edition consists of 5800 signed and numbered prints.

1979–80   FEDERAL DUCK STAMP
Green-Winged Teal   Lawrence K. Michaelsen

The original art is a 5″ × 7″ gouache painting of Green-Winged Teal in the water. It was chosen in open national competition from 374 entries.

The stamp was printed in full color and sold for $7.50. The first day of sale was July 1, 1979; 2,090,155 were sold.

The print is a 7″ × 9⅞″ four-color photolithograph, using Jefferies Custom Made Inks on Jefferies Archival 100 stock. The separation negative maker was Color Service (Los Angeles, CA), and the printer was Jefferies Bank Note Company. The first edition is 7000 regular plus 1500 with companion piece. The prints are numbered. In lieu of remarques, the artist here chose to produce miniature etchings the same size as the stamp, which can be framed alongside the stamp underneath the print.

1979 FIRST ALABAMA DUCK STAMP
Wood Ducks **Barbara Keel**

The original art depicts a pair of Wood Ducks standing on a log. The Alabama Department of Conservation commissioned the artist to design the artwork for this initial Alabama State Waterfowl Stamp.

The stamp is numbered on the front. It sold for $5.25. There were 35,000 stamps printed.

The print is 6½″ × 9″. The edition consists of 1750 signed and numbered prints. There are also 250 watercolor remarques.

1979 FIRST FLORIDA DUCK STAMP
Green-Winged Teal **Bob Binks**

The original art depicts a pair of Green-Winged Teal in flight. The Florida Game Commission commissioned the artist to design the artwork for this initial Florida State Duck Stamp.

The stamp is numbered on the front. It sold for $3.25. All of the 72,875 stamps that were printed were sold.

The print is 6″ × 9″. The edition consists of 1000 signed and numbered prints. There are, separately, also 250 watercolor remarques.

1979   FIRST MISSOURI DUCK STAMP
Giant Canada Geese   Charles W. Schwartz

The original art depicts three Giant Canada Geese coming in
for a landing. The Missouri Department of Conservation commissioned the artist to design the artwork for the state's first
waterfowl stamp.

The stamp is numbered on the front. It sold for $3.40. Of the
160,000 stamps that were printed, 56,694 were sold. The remainders were taken off sale on May 1, 1980.

The print is 6½″ × 9″. The edition consists of 2000 signed and
numbered prints, 200 of which are remarques.

1979 FIRST NEVADA DUCK STAMP
Tule Canvasback Decoy **Larry Hayden**

The original art depicts an ancient Tule Canvasback decoy used by the Northern Paiute Indians nearly 1000 years ago. The design was chosen from 32 entries in the open contest to determine the artwork for the state's first duck stamp. (The Nevada contest is open to residents of any state.)

The stamp is numbered on an attached booklet tab. It sold for $2.00. All of the 24,000 stamps that were printed were sold.

The print is 6½″ × 9″. The edition consists of 1990 signed and numbered prints, plus 500 pencil remarques.

1979   FIRST TENNESSEE DUCK STAMP
Mallards   **Dick Elliott**

The original art depicts three Mallards landing. The design was chosen from eleven entries in the state's open competition to choose a design for its initial waterfowl stamp. (The contest is open to residents of Tennessee only.)

The stamp is numbered on the front. It sold for $2.00|resident and $5.30 nonresident. The numbers printed were 60,000 resident and 20,000 nonresident. The numbers sold were 19,580 resident and 1491 nonresident. All remainders were taken off sale on June 30, 1981.

The print is 6⁷⁄₁₆″ × 8¹⁵⁄₁₆″. The edition consists of 1979 signed and numbered prints, 200 of which are remarques.

1980–81   FEDERAL DUCK STAMP
Mallards   **Richard W. Plasschaert**

The original art is a 5″ × 7″ rendering in acrylic of Mallards in flight. It was chosen in open national competition from 1329 entries.

The stamp was printed in full color and sold for $7.50. The first day of sale was July 1, 1980; 2,045,114 were sold.

The print is a 6½″ × 9″ four-color photolithograph, using special lite-fast inks on Rising Mirage stock. The separation negative maker and the printer was Johnson Printing, Inc. The first edition is 12,950 numbered but untitled prints.

1980 FIRST DELAWARE DUCK STAMP
Black Ducks Ned Mayne

The original art depicts a pair of Black Ducks in flight. The design was chosen from 35 entries in the open contest to determine the artwork for the state's first duck stamp. (The Delaware contest is open to residents of Delaware and also to residents of states that allow Delaware residents to enter their state contests.)

The stamp is not numbered (sheets were). It sold for $5.00. Of the 30,000 stamps that were printed, 17,510 were sold. The remainders were sold until July 1, 1983.

The print is 6½″ × 9″. The edition consists of 1980 signed and numbered prints, some of which have remarques in pencil.

DELAWARE MIGRATORY WATERFOWL STAMP

VOID AFTER JUNE 30, 1981

$5

1980 FIRST OKLAHOMA DUCK STAMP
Pintails **Patrick Sawyer**

The original art depicts a pair of Pintails in flight. The design was chosen from 89 entries in the open contest to determine the artwork for the state's first waterfowl stamp. (The contest is open to residents of Oklahoma only.)

The stamp is numbered on the back. It sold for $4.00. There were 60,000 stamps printed. Any remainders were sold until July 1, 1985.

The print is 6½″ × 9″. The edition consists of 1980 signed and numbered prints, some of which have remarques in color and some in pencil.

1981–82 FEDERAL DUCK STAMP
Ruddy Ducks **John S. Wilson**

The original art is a 5″ × 7″ gouache painting of the birds in the water. It was chosen in open national competition from 1507 entries.

The stamp was printed in full color and sold for $7.50. The first day of sale was July 1, 1981; 1,907,120 were sold. Note that individual stamps are separated only by the perforations in this unbordered design.

The print is a 6½″ × 9″ four-color photolithograph, using special lite-fast inks on Rives Offset stock. The separation negative maker and the printer was Johnson Printing, Inc. The first edition is 16,000 numbered but untitled prints. This stamp is different in that it is the first to have no defined borders. The tan background extends over the entire sheet, and the individual designs are separated only by the perforations.

1981   FIRST ARKANSAS DUCK STAMP
Mallards   **Lee LeBlanc**

The original art, entitled *Mallards in Flooded Timber*, depicts a flock of Mallards coming in for a landing. The Arkansas Fish and Game Department commissioned the artist to do the artwork for the state's initial waterfowl stamp. (No contests were held to determine artwork for later Arkansas designs.)

The stamp is numbered on the back. It sold for $5.50. Of the 200,000 stamps that were printed, 51,041 were sold. The remainders were sold until July 1, 1984.

The print is 6″ × 9″. The edition consists of 7200 signed and numbered prints. There are a separate Executive Edition of 500 and a remarqued edition of 600.

1981 FIRST SOUTH CAROLINA DUCK STAMP
Wood Ducks **Lee LeBlanc**

The original art depicts a pair of Wood Ducks standing on a log. The design was chosen from 56 entries in the open competition to determine the artwork for the state's first waterfowl stamp. (The South Carolina contest is open to residents of any state.)

The stamp is not numbered. It sold for $5.50. Of the 105,000 stamps that were printed, 36,022 were sold. The remainders were destroyed in April 1982.

The print is 6½″ × 9″. The edition consists of 4500 signed and numbered prints.

1981 FIRST TEXAS DUCK STAMP
Mallards **Larry Hayden**

The original art depicts a pair of Mallards swimming. The artist was state-appointed.

The stamp is numbered on the front. It sold for $5.00. Of the 300,000 stamps that were printed, 136,553 were sold. The remainders were destroyed on January 1, 1983.

The print is 6½″ × 9″. The edition consists of 16,500 signed and numbered prints.

1982–83 FEDERAL DUCK STAMP
Canvasbacks **David A. Maass**

The original art is a 5″ × 7″ oil-on-board painting of Canvasbacks in flight. It was chosen in open national competition from 2099 entries.

The stamp was printed in full color and sold for $7.50. The first day of sale was July 1, 1982; 1,926,253 were sold.

The print is a 6½″ × 9″ four-color photolithograph, using special lite-fast inks on Rag-Cote stock. The separation negative maker and the printer was Johnson Lithographics. The first edition comprises 22,250 numbered but untitled prints. There are also about 800 signed and numbered conservation prints that were donated to nonprofit wildlife-oriented organizations.

1982 FIRST NORTH DAKOTA DUCK STAMP
Giant Canada Geese   **Richard W. Plasschaert**

The original art depicts three Giant Canada Geese in flight. The North Dakota Game and Fish Department commissioned the artist to design the state's first annual stamp print. (In the future, the state will continue to commission only top-name artists to enhance the collectability of the stamps and prints.)

The stamp is numbered on the front. It sold for $9.00. There were 160,050 stamps printed. The remainders were sold until January 1, 1986.

The print is 6½″ × 9″. The edition consists of 9939 signed and numbered prints. There are also 250 artist's proofs.

1982   FIRST OHIO DUCK STAMP
Wood Ducks   **John A. Ruthven**

The original art depicts a pair of Wood Ducks in flight. The Ohio Fish and Game Department commissioned the artist to design the artwork for the first state waterfowl stamp.

The stamp is not numbered. It sold for $5.75. Of the 100,000 stamps that were printed, 41,309 were sold. The remainders were sold until January 1, 1984.

The print is 6½″ × 9″. The edition consists of 9000 signed and numbered prints. There are, separately, 530 pencil remarques and 300 color remarques.

1983–84 FEDERAL DUCK STAMP
Untitled (Pintails) **Phil Scholer**

The original art is a 5″ × 7″ rendering in acrylic of Pintails in the water. It was chosen in open national competition from 1564 entries.

The stamp was printed in full color and sold for $7.50. The first day of sale was July 1, 1983; 1,867,998 were sold.

The print is a 6½″ × 9″ photolithograph, in five colors, using special lite-fast inks on Rising Mirage stock. The separation negative maker and the printer was Mueller-Krus. The first edition consists of 17,400 regular prints and a separately numbered edition of 6700 prints accompanying a gold-plated medallion commemorating the fiftieth duck stamp.

1983 FIRST NEW HAMPSHIRE DUCK STAMP
Wood Ducks   **Richard W. Plasschaert**

The original art depicts a pair of Wood Ducks in flight. Mr. Plasschaert became the first artist to design three "first-of-state" waterfowl stamp prints when he was commissioned to do this design.

The stamp is numbered on the front. It sold for $4.00. There were 100,000 printed. The remainders were destroyed on April 1, 1984.

The print is 6½″ × 9″. The edition consists of 5507 signed and numbered prints. There are, separately, 400 artist's proofs.

1983 NH MIGRATORY WATERFOWL STAMP

$4.00

WOOD DUCKS

1983 FIRST NORTH CAROLINA DUCK STAMP
Mallards   **Richard W. Plasschaert**

The original art depicts a pair of Mallards landing on the water. The artist was selected by bid proposal to design the state's initial stamp.

The stamp is not numbered. It sold for $5.50. There were 100,000 stamps printed. The remainders were sold until June 30, 1984.

The print is 6½" × 9". The edition consists of 13,652 signed and numbered prints.

WATERFOWL CONSERVATION STAMP

1983 NORTH CAROLINA

$5.50

1983 FIRST PENNSYLVANIA DUCK STAMP
Sycamore Creek Woodies   **Ned Smith**

The original art depicts a pair of Wood Ducks in flight. The artist was commissioned to design the artwork.

The stamp is not numbered. It sold for $5.50. There were 55,000 stamps printed. The remainders were sold until December 31, 1984.

The print is 6½" × 9". The edition consists of 7380 signed and numbered prints. There are also 625 gold medallions.

90

1984–85 FEDERAL DUCK STAMP
Untitled (Widgeon)   **William C. Morris**

The original art is a 5″ × 7″ acrylic watercolor painting of Widgeon in the water. It was chosen in open national competition from 1582 entries.

The stamp was printed in full color and sold for $7.50. The first day of sale was July 2, 1984; 1,913,509 were sold.

The print is a 6½″ × 9″ four-color photolithograph, using special lite-fast inks on Rising Mirage stock. The separation negative maker and the printer was Mueller-Krus. The first edition consists of 20,400 regular and 11,500 with companion piece. The prints are numbered but not titled. In addition to the regular edition and companion edition, an edition of 500 remarqued prints was issued. They were available only with a matching numbered remarqued 1984 Alabama Duck Stamp print, which was also the work of the artist William C. Morris.

1984 FIRST MAINE DUCK STAMP
Black Ducks   David A. Maass

The original art depicts a pair of Black Ducks in flight. The artist was selected by bid proposal.

The stamp is numbered on the front. It sold for $2.50. There were 60,000 stamps printed. The remainders were sold until July 1, 1985.

The print is 6½″ × 9″. The edition consists of 11,115 signed and numbered prints and 1730 gold medallions.

1984 MAINE MIGRATORY WATERFOWL STAMP

1984 FIRST NEW JERSEY DUCK STAMP
Canvasbacks **Thomas Hirata**

The original art depicts a pair of Canvasbacks swimming in calm water. The artist was chosen by bid competition.

The stamp is numbered on the front. It sold for $2.50 resident and $5.00 nonresident. The number of stamps printed was 102,000 resident and 102,000 nonresident. The remainders were sold until December 31, 1985.

The print is 6½″ × 9″. The edition consists of 10,011 signed and numbered prints with 1210 gold medallions. There is an Executive Edition with 650 color remarques and gold medallions. There are 150 artist's proofs, numbered separately, with color remarques and gold medallions.

1984   FIRST OREGON DUCK STAMP
Canada Geese   **Michael Sieve**

The original art depicts Canada Geese in flight.

The stamp is numbered on the front. It sold for $5.00. There were 120,000 stamps printed. The remainders were sold until June 30, 1985.

The print, entitled *Dusky Canada Geese*, is 6½″ × 9″. The edition consists of 11,825 signed and numbered prints. There are also 2975 silver medallions.

1984 Oregon Waterfowl Stamp

1985–86 FEDERAL DUCK STAMP
Untitled (Cinnamon Teal) **Gerald Mobley**

The original art is a 5″ × 7″ opaque watercolor painting of a Cinnamon Teal drake in its spring plumage gliding on calm water. It was chosen in open national competition from 1515 entries.

The stamp was printed in full color and sold for $7.50. The first day of sale was July 1, 1985; 1,779,299 were sold.

The print is a 6½″ × 9″ four-color photolithograph, using special lite-fast inks on acid-free Rising Mirage stock. The separation negative maker and the printer was Mueller-Krus. The first edition consists of 18,200 regular prints and 6650 with companion piece. The prints are signed and numbered but not titled. A Medallion Edition of 6650, consisting of a matching numbered print and a gold-plated medallion, were also made available.

U.S. DEPARTMENT OF THE INTERIOR

MIGRATORY BIRD HUNTING AND CONSERVATION STAMP

$7.50

CINNAMON TEAL · VOID AFTER JUNE 30, 1986

95

1985 FIRST ALASKA DUCK STAMP
Emperor Geese   Daniel Smith

The original art depicts a trio of Emperor Geese standing in the snow. For this first-of-state Alaska Duck Stamp, the Alaska Fish and Game Department selected Mr. Smith to create the design.

The stamp is numbered on the back. It sold for $5.00. There were 130,020 stamps printed.

The print is 6½″ × 9″. The edition consists of 14,650 signed and numbered prints and 2450 gold-plated medallions with prints. Also available was an Executive Edition of 250, consisting of print with color remarque and medallion.

1985 Alaska Waterfowl Stamp

1985 FIRST GEORGIA DUCK STAMP
Wood Ducks   Daniel Smith

The original art was chosen from 37 entries. Mr. Smith, who also won the 1985 Alaska competition, is the first artist to win two first-of-state competitions in the same year.

The stamp is not numbered. It sold for $5.50. There were 105,020 stamps printed.

The print is 6½″ × 9″. The edition consists of 14,100 signed and numbered prints. Also available were a Medallion Edition of 1460 and an Executive Edition of 250, consisting of print, medallion, and color remarque.

1985 FIRST GEORGIA WATERFOWL CONSERVATION STAMP

$5.50

1985   FIRST KENTUCKY DUCK STAMP
Mallards   **Ray Harm**

The original art for this first-of-state design depicts a pair of
Mallards coming in for a landing over the trees. The design
was commissioned from the artist.

The stamp is numbered on the front. It sold for $5.25. There
were 45,000 stamps printed.

The print is 6½" × 9". The edition consists of 8189 signed and
numbered prints. Added to this were 566 signed and numbered prints with gold medallion, 60 signed and numbered
prints with medallion and pencil remarque, and 273 signed
and numbered prints with medallion and color remarque.

1985   FIRST NEW YORK DUCK STAMP
Canada Geese   **Larry Barton**

The original art depicts a flock of Canada Geese in flight. The artist was selected to create the design.

The stamp is numbered on the front. It sold for $5.50. There were 200,010 stamps printed.

The print is 6½″ × 9″. The edition consisted of 14,040 signed and numbered prints; 1035 silver medallions were also available. Also available were an Executive Edition of 580, consisting of print, medallion, and remarque, and an Artist's Proof Edition of 250, consisting of artist's proof print, medallion, and remarque.

1985 FIRST WYOMING DUCK STAMP
Canada Geese **Robert Kusserow**

The original art depicts three Canada Geese by the water's edge. It was chosen from 30 entries.

The stamp, printed in full color, is numbered on the front and sold for $5.00. There were 450,000 printed.

The print measures 6½″ × 9″. The edition consists of 4750 signed and numbered prints. In addition there is an Executive Edition of 250 prints plus 250 artist's proofs with remarques.

WYOMING 1985 Conservation Stamp

Expires December 31, 1985

SIGNATURE

1986–87 FEDERAL DUCK STAMP
Fulvous Whistling Duck **Burton E. Moore, Jr.**

The original art is an acrylic-on-Masonite painting of a Fulvous Whistling Duck in the water. ("Fulvous" refers to the duck's deep yellow or tawny color.) The design was chosen from 1242 entries.

The stamp, which was unnumbered, was printed in full color and sold for $7.50. The first day of sale was July 1, 1986. Four million were printed; it is not known how many were sold.

The print, 6½″ × 9″, is acrylic on Masonite, using fade-resistant inks on 100% acid-free rag stock. The separation negative maker and printer was Mueller-Krus. The first edition consists of 16,310 prints. Also available was a Medallion Edition of 4670, consisting of a matching numbered print and a gold-plated medallion.

U.S. DEPARTMENT OF THE INTERIOR

1986 FIRST MONTANA WATERFOWL STAMP
Canada Geese Joe Thornbrugh

The original art depicts a flock of Canada Geese flying over mountainous terrain. The design for this first-of-state water-fowl stamp was chosen from 60 entries.

The stamp is numbered on the front. It sold for $5.00. There were 70,000 stamps printed.

The print is 6½″ × 9″. The edition consists of 9212 signed and numbered prints. Also available were a Medallion Edition consisting of 1025 prints and gold-plated medallions, and an Executive Edition consisting of 300 matching prints, gold-plated medallions, and color remarques hand-painted by the artist.

1986 FIRST SOUTH DAKOTA WATERFOWL RESTORATION STAMP
Canada Geese   **John S. Wilson**

The original art was chosen from 42 entries. The South Dakota legislature passed a law requiring that waterfowl hunters have this Waterfowl Restoration Stamp.

The stamp is numbered on the front. It sold for $2.00. There were 135,000 stamps printed.

The print is 6½″ × 9″. The edition consists of 950 signed and numbered prints; pencil remarques were also available with this edition.

SOUTH DAKOTA WATERFOWL RESTORATION STAMP

1986   FIRST UTAH WATERFOWL STAMP
Tundra Swans   **Leon Parson**

The original art depicts a pair of Tundra Swans in flight. The design for this first-of-state waterfowl stamp was chosen from 61 entries.

The stamp is numbered on the front. It sold for $3.30. There were 120,000 stamps printed.

The print is 6½″ × 9″. The edition consists of 14,028 signed and numbered prints. Also available were a Silver Medallion Edition of 1600, a Gold Medallion Edition of 250, and a Color Remarqued Edition of 150.

FIRST OF STATE 1986 Exp. 6-30-87

1986 FIRST VERMONT DUCK STAMP
Wood Ducks **Jim Killen**

The original art depicts a trio of Wood Ducks in flight. The artist was commissioned to create the design.

The stamp is not numbered. It sold for $5.00. There were 50,000 stamps printed.

The print is 6½″ × 9″. The edition consists of 13,910 signed and numbered prints. Also available were a Gold Medallion Edition of 1590 and an Executive Edition of 195, consisting of print, medallion, and color remarque.

1986 FIRST WASHINGTON DUCK STAMP
Mallards **Keith Warrick**

The original art depicts a pair of Mallards resting on a snow-covered shoreline. The design was chosen from 109 entries.

The stamp is numbered on the front. It sold for $5.00. There were 160,000 stamps printed.

The print is 6½″ × 9″. The edition consists of 12,180 signed and numbered prints. Also available were a Gold Medallion Edition of 1775 and an Executive Edition of 300, consisting of print, medallion, and color remarque.

1987–88 FEDERAL DUCK STAMP
Redheads **Arthur G. Anderson**

The original art depicts the flight of three Redheads sweeping across a backwater marsh. It was chosen from 798 entries.

The stamp, which is unnumbered, was printed in full color and sold for $10.00. Four million were printed. The first day of sale was July 1, 1987.

The print, 6½" × 9", is on 100% acid-free rag stock. The separation maker was Graphic Arts Systems and the printer was Overland Printer. The first edition consists of 20,000 prints. In addition to the regular edition, there was a Medallion Edition of 5000 gold-plated, stamp-shaped medallions accompanied by a print.

107

1987   FIRST ARIZONA DUCK STAMP
Pintail   Daniel Smith

The original art depicts a pair of Pintails swimming in the water. The design was chosen from 21 entries.

The stamp (as well as the sheet) is numbered. It sold for $5.50. There were 70,500 printed, 30,000 in books and the rest in sheets.

The print is 6½″ × 9″. The edition consisted of 10,400 signed and numbered prints. Added to this were a Medallion Edition of 1390, consisting of stamp, print, and gold-plated medallion, and an Executive Edition of 198, consisting of stamp, medallion, and print with hand-painted color remarque.

1987 FIRST IDAHO DUCK STAMP
Untitled **Robert Leslie**

The original art depicts a pair of Cinnamon Teal in the water. The design for this first-of-state stamp/print was chosen from 40 entries.

The stamp sold for $6.00. There were 80,000 printed.

The print is 6½″ × 9″. The edition of signed and numbered prints is limited to orders received by April 1988. A companion print of 16½″ × 25″ was also available. Also issued were a Medallion Edition and an Executive Edition consisting of print, medallion, and hand-painted color remarque.

54- 024687

1987-88
EXPIRES
JUNE 30, 1988

IDAHO $5.50

MIGRATORY WATERFOWL STAMP

1987   FIRST KANSAS DUCK STAMP
Green-Winged Teal   **Guy Coheleach**

The original art depicts a pair of Green-Winged Teal taking off from marshy water. The design for this first-of-state stamp/print was commissioned.

The stamp is numbered and sold for $3.00. There were 100,000 printed.

The print is 6½″ × 9″. The edition of signed and numbered prints is limited to the orders received through February 1988. A Medallion Edition of 2500 was also available, consisting of a print using the same paper as that used for the signed and numbered edition and a gold-plated medallion facsimile of the stamp. Also available was an Executive Etching Edition of 950 hand-colored 6½″ × 9″ etchings by the artist, a medallion, mint stamp, and portfolio.

1987 KANSAS Waterfowl Habitat Stamp

$3

001199

Exp. 6-30-88

50th Year-DUCKS UNLIMITED

1987 FIRST WEST VIRGINIA DUCK STAMP
Canada Geese   **Daniel Smith**

The original art depicts a pair of Canada Geese in flight. The design was commissioned.

The stamp, which is unnumbered, sold for $5.00. There were 58,000 printed.

The print is 6½″ × 9″. The edition consists of 10,064 signed and numbered prints. Added to that were a Gold Medallion Edition of 1101 and an Executive Edition of 145, consisting of resident and nonresident stamps, color remarqued print, and medallion.

1988–89 FEDERAL DUCK STAMP
Untitled **Daniel Smith**

The original art depicts a Snow Goose in early morning flight over a marsh. The design was chosen from 844 entries.

The stamp is not numbered, and it sold for $10.00. Four million stamps were printed. The first day of sale was July 1, 1988.

The print was made using fade-resistant inks on 100 percent acid-free rag paper. The size of the image is 6½″ × 9″, and the edition consists of 22,000 prints. In addition to the regular edition, there are editions which included silver and gold medallions and 14-karat solid gold medallions.

1988 FIRST VIRGINIA DUCK STAMP
Chesapeake Country Mallards   **Ronald J. Louque**

The original art depicts a pair of Mallards landing in a marsh. It was chosen in a contest from more than a dozen entries.

The stamp, which was numbered, sold for $5.00. There were 60,000 stamps printed, and they were sold for eighteen months. The remainders were destroyed.

The print is 6½" × 9". The edition consists of 14,500 signed and numbered prints. There are also separate editions which include gold-plated medallions, artist's proof prints, and pencil and color remarques.

113

ARTISTS' BIOGRAPHIES

JACKSON MILES ABBOTT
1957–58 Federal Duck Stamp

Jackson Miles Abbott was born in Philadelphia on January 25, 1920. He started at age six with the hobby of ornithology and still maintains a very active interest in the subject. During World War II, Mr. Abbott was in military engineering and pursued a career in both the Army and the civil service. But over the years, he has made birds the focus of his art. In 1957 he won both first and second place in the Federal Duck Stamp competition and since that year has conducted an annual nesting survey of the bald eagle population in the Chesapeake Bay region for the Audubon Society and the U.S. Fish and Wildlife Service. As well as writing and illustrating articles on birds for books and magazines, he has written and illustrated a Sunday magazine column on the birds in Washington, D.C. Some of his writing and illustration can be found in Austin's *New Encyclopedia of Useful Information* (1948) and Hausman's *Beginner's Guide to Attracting Birds* (1951).

ARTHUR G. ANDERSON
1987–88 Federal Duck Stamp

Arthur G. Anderson was born in Eau Claire, Wisconsin, on December 10, 1935. At the early age of twelve, he began painting with a set of oils his uncle gave to him. Mr. Anderson studied art at the University of Wisconsin at Eau Claire and also at the Art Instruction School in St. Paul, Minnesota. He supported himself as a graphic artist while continuing to paint at home on evenings and weekends. In 1983, he began to devote his full time to wildlife art. An avid outdoorsman, Mr. Anderson admits he "hunts mostly with his camera." He lives with his family now in Onalaska, Wisconsin, a town near La Crosse that overlooks the Mississippi and is close to the marsh habitat frequented by ducks and other waterfowl in their annual migrations. In 1985, he gained international recognition when his painting "Riding the Wind" was selected as one of the companion pieces to the Ducks Unlimited Artist of the Year painting.

LARRY BARTON
1985 New York Duck Stamp

Larry Barton grew up on the shores of Lake Huron in the Michigan "thumb" region, where he early developed an interest in wildlife. He continued this interest by studying wildlife biology and management. He also pursued a journalism career, becoming a popular award-winning editorial cartoonist whose works have appeared in such publications as *Time*, the *Washington Post*, the *New York Times*, and the *Los Angeles Times* as well as newspapers in Ohio and North Carolina. He was able to return to wildlife painting full-time in 1979, and has steadily gained recognition. His artwork has appeared in many prestigious shows and galleries, and in the Leigh Yawkey Woodson Art Museum. He lives in North Carolina with his wife and family.

JUSTUS H. ("SONNY") BASHORE
1976 Indiana Duck Stamp

Justus H. ("Sonny") Bashore was born in Paulding, Ohio, on November 12, 1935. He served in the armed forces following high school, and on his return to civilian life, he began his career with the Ohio Department of Natural Resources. He worked as a wildlife artist and area manager at the Oxbow Lake Wildlife Area at Defiance, Ohio, and served with the Indiana Department of Natural Resources at Curtis Creek Trout and Salmon Station at Mongo, Indiana. He continues to paint and carve as a full-time wildlife artist. In 1977 he placed first in the Indiana Trout and Salmon Stamp competition. In 1987 he was the winner in the First Annual Michigan Duck Hunters' Tournament and Midwest Decoy Contest Poster competition.

FRANK WESTON BENSON
1935–36 Federal Duck Stamp

Frank Weston Benson, M.A., was born in Salem, Massachusetts, on March 24, 1862. When he was eighteen he began his art studies at the Boston Museum of Fine Arts. Three years later, in 1883, he went to Paris to study at the Academie Julien under Boulanger and Lefebvre. On his return in 1885, Mr. Benson taught painting and drawing and continued with his own work, painting portraits that featured his subjects out of doors in scenes of brilliant light and color. In 1912, he took up etching and afterwards made over three hundred plates, which gained wide acclaim for his work. As he developed, his style became more noted for simplicity and sparseness of detail. It is a style more appreciated by the expert than the layman, as it makes a statement so bare and brief that only the most technically competent artist could bring it off. Mr. Benson died in 1951 at the age of eighty-nine.

EDWARD J. BIERLY
1956–57 Federal Duck Stamp, 1963–64 Federal Duck Stamp,
1970–71 Federal Duck Stamp

Edward J. Bierly was born in 1920, in Buffalo, New York. His job as a designer of natural history exhibits for the National Park Service led to an appointment by UNESCO as a museum consultant to the government of Rhodesia. It was on this assignment that he first saw the wildlife of Africa. Moved by what he saw, he determined to use his art to attract attention to the plight of endangered fauna everywhere. In 1970 he left the Park Service to devote his full time to his art. His paintings have appeared on the covers of national magazines and have been exhibited at natural history museums throughout the country. Many of his print editions have been used to raise funds for wildlife conservation programs. He is a three-time winner of the Federal Duck Stamp competition and a member of the Society of Animal Artists.

BOB BINKS
1979 Florida Duck Stamp

Robert Binks was born in St. Louis, Missouri, on September 19, 1941. From his earliest memories he has always been vitally interested in wildlife. Mr. Binks began his working career as a technical illustrator and gradually went into advertising. While working at his then fulltime job as art director, he never lost sight of his real love—wildlife art. A self-taught artist, he was commissioned to design the first duck stamp for the state of Florida in 1979. In 1982 he won the competition for the South Carolina Duck Stamp, and in 1985 he again designed the Florida Duck Stamp. He has given numerous one-man shows, and exhibited at Easton's Waterfowl Festival and at the National Waterfowl Art Show in Kansas City. He was also selected as Artist of the Year for Florida's Ducks Unlimited.

RICHARD E. BISHOP
1936–37 Federal Duck Stamp

Richard E. Bishop was born in Syracuse, New York, on May 30, 1887. Early in his career at a manufacturing plant, he found himself faced with a pile of inviting copper plates. With a phonograph needle, on a waxed plate, he inscribed the first of his many etchings. Mr. Bishop traveled widely in search of wildlife material, joining two African safaris organized by the American Museum of Natural History and also making trips to Great Britain, the Pacific Islands, and North and South America. His decorated glassware and china are highly regarded, but the books of his etchings are most widely cherished. Among these are *Bishop's Birds* (1936), *Bishop's Waterfowl* (1948), and *Prairie Wings* (1962) in collaboration with Edgar M. Queeny. Mr. Bishop rendered wildlife in many media: watercolors, oil paintings, aquatints, dry points, etchings, jewelry, tiles, metal, glassware, and china. He died in 1975.

WALTER E. BOHL
1943–44 Federal Duck Stamp

Walter E. Bohl was born in Columbus, Wisconsin, on September 10, 1907. In 1931 and 1932, when he was recovering from a serious illness, he began making pen and ink drawings, just to pass the time. At the suggestion of the manager of the Marshall Field Art Galleries of Chicago he turned to making etchings. Because he loved the outdoors, it was natural that his subjects were birds, animals, and outdoor scenes. In 1935, some of his work came to the attention of *Esquire*, which featured his etchings and paintings for nine years. With no formal art education, he has firmly established his reputation as an etcher and painter. Some of his etchings can be found in the permanent collection of the Smithsonian National Museum of American Art, Washington, D.C. His etchings are also in collections of Arizona State University, Tempe, Arizona, the University of Wisconsin at Madison, and the State House, Phoenix, Arizona. His paintings are in the collection of the Phoenix Art Museum, Phoenix, Arizona. In 1971 he was awarded a gold medal by the Arizona Chapter of the National Society of Arts and Letters.

ROLAND H. CLARK
1938–39 Federal Duck Stamp

Roland H. Clark was born in New Rochelle, New York, on April 2, 1874. He attended private schools in New York City and received his formal art education under tutors at the Art Students League. Mr. Clark lived for 22 years in Gloucester, Virginia, on an offshoot of Chesapeake Bay. He went into oystering as a business, but he found too many opportunities there for wildlife painting to be diverted for long. He is principally noted for some five hundred etchings he did of game birds and wildfowl, but he has done oil paintings of sporting scenes and watercolors as well. In addition, he wrote four books —mostly recollections of his hunting trips—all illustrated by himself. He was a charter member of the American Sporting Artists and also a member of Ducks Unlimited, Inc. He died in Norwalk, Connecticut, on April 13, 1957.

GUY COHELEACH
1987 Kansas Duck Stamp

Guy Coheleach was born in New York. He has been in the forefront of contemporary wildlife art for the last thirty years. He is listed in *Who's Who in the World*, *Who's Who in America*, and *Who's Who in American Art*. His work has been exhibited in the National Collection of Fine Art, the White House, and the Royal Ontario Museum. Incidentally, he was the first American artist to exhibit in Beijing, China. Among his honors was his selection in 1983 as Master Artist of the Year by the Leigh Yawkey Woodson Art Museum. Visiting heads of state have received his eagle print.

ARTHUR M. COOK
1972–73 Federal Duck Stamp

Arthur M. Cook was born in Oak Park, Illinois, on September 15, 1931. At the age of ten, he moved with his family to the Minneapolis area. He began his formal art studies in high school and pursued them through Hamline University and the Minneapolis School of Art. He held a number of positions in commercial art with different studios and is now industrial art director at Honeywell. Always an active conservationist, he is a member of both the National and International Wildlife Federations, Ducks Unlimited, the National Audubon Society, and Trout Unlimited. He has also found time to gain recognition as a lily hybridizer and do botanical drawings for the North American Lily Society Yearbook. He loves hunting and fishing and always brings a camera with him to do research for his wildlife paintings.

JAY NORWOOD DARLING
1934–35 Federal Duck Stamp

Jay Norwood ("Ding") Darling was born on October 21, 1876, in Norwood, Michigan, which gave him his middle name. He early acquired the nickname "Ding," and it stuck. His art career began during a stint as a reporter on the Sioux City Tribune, where he began cartooning. In 1906, he took a job with the Des Moines Register and Tribune, where he stayed until his retirement in 1949. Beginning in 1917, his cartoons were syndicated in 130 daily newspapers, and his drawings were compiled and published in a book every two years from 1908 to 1920. In 1934, he designed the first duck stamp himself. He received many honors over the years, including two Pulitzer Prizes for journalism, two honorary doctorates, and other medals and awards. Mr. Darling died in 1962.

JOHN HENRY DICK
1952–53 Federal Duck Stamp

John Henry Dick was born in Islip, New York, on May 12, 1919. As a child he did not take up drawing but maintained a respectable collection of wildfowl. In 1947, Mr. Dick moved to a plantation in South Carolina that had belonged to his mother. There he began his first professional drawings of birds. At that time, he worked on commissions and as the illustrator for numerous magazines and books. Photography, another of his interests, has taken him throughout the world to take pictures of birds and animals. His works have appeared in *The Bird Watchers of America, Carolina Low Country Impressions, A Gathering of Shore Birds, Florida Bird Life*, and *South Carolina Bird Life*, as well as *A Pictorial Guide to the Birds of India* and *The Birds of China*. Throughout, Mr. Dick has maintained aviaries and closed pens of birds at Dixie Plantation.

DICK ELLIOTT
1979 Tennessee Duck Stamp

Dick Elliott was born on November 30, 1931. A graduate of Austin Peay State College and the Harris School of Art, he is a professional illustrator and designer. Mr. Elliott has had years of experience in the art field both as a teacher at the University of Tennessee and as a commercial art director for the Methodist Publishing House and Genesco in Nashville. Crisp, bright watercolors are the hallmark of his work, and he is adept at blending the designs of nature and of man into one unified piece. His landscapes and life portraits bring a vivid and refreshing style to contemporary subjects. Mr. Elliott is a member of the Tennessee Watercolor Society and has had numerous exhibitions and one-man shows. He now resides in Hendersonville, just outside Nashville.

ROBERT ESCHENFELDT
1975 Illinois Duck Stamp

Robert Eschenfeldt was born on October 14, 1930. He is a graduate of Chicago's American Academy of Art. For the past twenty years, Mr. Eschenfeldt has worked as an illustrator and an art director. He prides himself in capturing detail and accuracy in his paintings.

JAMES P. FISHER
1975–76 Federal Duck Stamp

James P. Fisher was born in Wilmington, Delaware, on February 25, 1912. At the age of seventeen, while attending art school, he decided that if he was to succeed in his goal of becoming an artist, he would have to work harder. He took on the task of copying each of the plates from E.S. Thompson's *Art Anatomy of Animals*. Completing this project indelibly printed on his mind the importance of anatomical knowledge in drawing. He spent three years at the Wilmington Academy of Art, and after that he turned to commercial advertising art for his livelihood. He kept, however, his old interest in wildlife. A fascination with old derelict decoys prompted him to go to a decoy show in 1973, where he met a collector who allowed him to borrow from his collection for painting. Out of this came his first and only entry in the Federal Duck Stamp contest.

ALBERT EARL GILBERT
1978–79 Federal Duck Stamp

Albert Earl ("Gil") Gilbert was born in Chicago on August 22, 1939. His favorite place as a boy was the Brookfield Zoo, where he often skipped school to sketch animals and birds. After a brief stint as a park ranger, he began his career as a wildlife artist, doing illustrations for nature magazines and painting many of the National Wildlife Federation's stamps. Working with the American Museum of Natural History, he illustrated several books including *Eagles, Hawks and Falcons of the World*. Mr. Gilbert served as president of the Society of Animal Artists from 1977 through 1984. He was the first artist to paint full-color remarques for the Federal Duck Stamp prints. Originals of some of his works can be found in the Carnegie Museum, the Field Museum, and the Princeton University Art Museum. Mr. Gilbert was honored wth a chapter on his art in the recently published book *Twentieth-Century Wildlife Artists*. Possibly his most widely published artwork is the wild turkey he painted many years ago for the Wild Turkey Bourbon label.

OWEN J. GROMME
1945–46 Federal Duck Stamp, 1978 Wisconsin Duck Stamp

Owen J. Gromme was born in Fond du Lac, Wisconsin, on July 5, 1968. Early on he was a hunter and outdoorsman, and his work reflects the great interest he always had in birds. During his years at the Milwaukee Public Museum, Mr. Gromme went on several expeditions, including several to Alaska and another to the Hudson Bay area. He also went in 1928 and 1929 to Africa, a trip that began his serious work in painting. Some of his paintings illustrated *Birds of Wisconsin* (1963); other publications featuring his work include *The Wild Turkey*, the book jacket and cover of *Birds Will Come to You, Circus World Museum, Baraboo, Wisconsin*, and several plates in *Birds of Colorado*. Mr. Gromme also provided a complete gallery of paintings for the Marshal & Ilsey Bank of Milwaukee, and a hall in the Milwaukee Public Museum was named in his honor.

RAY HARM
1985 Kentucky Duck Stamp

Ray Harm was born in 1926, in Randolph County, West Virginia. His interest in wildlife began early in his life in West Virginia, where his father, who made a living digging and drying mountain herbs, taught him much. In his teen years, he traveled west, working as a ranch hand and as a rodeo rider. He then returned east to study at the Cooper School of Art and the Cleveland Institute of Art. Besides the recognition he has earned as a wildlife painter, he is also a lecturer and nature writer. Mr. Harm was also one of the two founders, in 1961, of what is known today as the limited edition print industy, and it was natural for him to be commissioned to do the design for the First of State Kentucky Duck Stamp. Mr. Harm currently operates a ranch southeast of Tucson, Arizona.

LARRY HAYDEN
1979 Nevada Duck Stamp, 1981 Texas Duck Stamp

Larry Hayden was born in Detroit, Michigan, on March 21, 1934. An avid hunter and fisherman, he found it only natural to turn his artistic talents to his favorite pastime—waterfowl. Long recognized as one of the premier competitive decoy carvers, Mr. Hayden mixes both avocations; for instance, his hen Canvasback in the 1977 Michigan design is painted from the same reference material he used to carve the decoy that won Best of Show in the 1977 World Decoy Carving Championships. His works are very much in demand, with both his Duck Stamp prints and his annual "Marsh Duck" series being immediate sellouts. He was commissioned by bid selection to design the 1981 First of State Texas Stamp. Mr. Hayden is a full-time wildlife artist who lives with his wife and family in Framington Hills, Michigan.

ROBERT W. HINES
1946–47 Federal Duck Stamp

Robert W. Hines was born in Columbus, Ohio, on February 6, 1912. Early in 1939, he was accepted as a staff artist for the Ohio Division of Conservation. Nine years later, he became an artist with the U.S. Fish and Wildlife Service in Washington. He illustrated *The Edge of the Sea* by Rachel Carson, his first supervisor at the Wildlife Service. Because he was working for a scientific organization, he had to make his art extremely accurate, and his drawings and paintings have been reproduced by conservation magazines in every state of the Union, in Canada, and even in the Soviet Union. He wrote and illustrated *Ducks at a Distance*. Moreover, Mr. Hines has done illustrations for more than eighty books and publications and has painted four wildlife murals for the Interior Building in Washington, D.C.

THOMAS HIRATA
1984 New Jersey Duck Stamp

Thomas Hirata was born in Passaic, New Jersey, on January 11, 1955. His paintings, strong in design, reflect his tight, realistic approach to painting oil on board. Most of his works involve several textures and various lighting techniques. He received his formal art training from Colorado College in Colorado Springs, the Art Students League in New York City, and the Art Center College of Design in Pasadena, California. His work has been exhibited in shows at the Leigh Yawkey Woodson Art Museum, the Smithsonian, the Denver Museum of Natural History, and other shows throughout the United States. A member of the Society of Animal Artists and Ducks Unlimited, Mr. Hirata currently resides in Rutherford, New Jersey.

LYNN BOGUE HUNT, SR.
1939–40 Federal Duck Stamp

Lynn Bogue Hunt was born in 1878, in Honeoye Falls, New York. At the age of twelve, he went to Michigan to live and continued his strong interest in the study and drawing of wildlife. He also developed skills in taxidermy. After three years in college, Mr. Hunt became a staff artist at the *Detroit Free Press*. At the same time, he began sending wildlife artwork to various national magazines and soon moved to New York, where he continued to sell more and more of his work. He published in such magazines as *Saturday Evening Post*, *Field and Stream*, *Natural History*, and many others. In 1936, he published a book of bird paintings and drawings, *An Artist's Game Bag*. His illustrations also appeared in *A Book on Duck Shooting*, *American Big Game Fishing*, *Atlantic Big Game Fishing*, *American Neighbors of the Countryside*, *American Hunter*, and others. Mr. Hunt died in 1960.

FRANCIS LEE JAQUES
1940–41 Federal Duck Stamp

Francis Lee Jaques was born in Geneseo, Illinois, on September 28, 1887. Although he began his career as an artist at age thirty-three, if all his works were put together they would total close to thirty thou-

sand square feet, an outstanding amount. In 1924, he joined the American Museum of Natural History where he produced a multitude of background paintings that can still be seen in many American museums. Mr. Jaques illustrated a number of books produced in collaboration with his wife, Florence Sarah Page, a writer. His illustrations appeared in other books, too, among them *Oceanic Birds of South America*, *American South Carolina Bird Life*, *Florida Bird Life*, and *Outdoor Life's Gallery of North American Game*. In addition, Mr. Jaques and his wife received the John Burroughs Medal, an award for the best nature study books. Mr. Jaques is deceased.

RON JENKINS
1965–66 Federal Duck Stamp

Ron Jenkins was born in Pawtucket, Rhode Island, on August 18, 1932. After service in the Marines for three years, he attended the Philadelphia Museum of Art in 1955. He had to leave art study for a paying job, but he maintained his painting, and in 1964 he won the Federal Duck Stamp contest. Mr. Jenkins began freelancing in 1966. He has illustrations in *Pennsylvania Game News*, *Pennsylvania Angler*, *National Geographic*, and *Modern Game Breeding*. Mr. Jenkins works in any medium, but has said that the fast-drying media of opaque watercolor and polymer suit him best. He also teaches from time to time and gives lectures on art and conservation. Mr. Jenkins makes his home in Missoula, Montana.

PAUL B. JOHNSON
1971 California Duck Stamp

Paul Johnson was born in San Francisco on February 18, 1907. He attended the San Francisco School of Arts on a scholarship he won with his drawing and sculpture. He was the wildlife artist on contract for the California Department of Fish and Game from 1952 to 1985. His wildlife designs have been featured in many publications, including the *Outdoor California* magazine, which is the Fish and Game Department's bimonthly publication. The only artist to be commissioned to do more than one state duck stamp design, he was asked to do the art for the first seven California waterfowl stamps.

EDWIN RICHARD KALMBACH
1941–42 Federal Duck Stamp

Edwin Richard Kalmbach, D. Sc., was born in Grand Rapids, Michigan, on April 29, 1884. His first job was as assistant director of the Kent Science Museum. He then worked as a biologist in the Biological Survey, a forerunner of the Fish and Wildlife Service. He did many field studies on the crow, blackbird, house sparrow, starling, magpie, and other wildlife. He was deeply involved in dealing with a baffling malady of Western waterfowl; his research led to the discovery of avian botulism, which formed the basis of a campaign against duck sickness. Dr. Kalmbach received the Leopold Medal of the Wildlife Society, and he was the recipient of the highest honor of the Department of the Interior—the Distinguished Service Award. Dr. Kalmbach is deceased.

BARBARA KEEL
1979 Alabama Duck Stamp

Barbara Keel was born in Opelika, Alabama. She has spent many hours around her home studying the abundant wildlife of the area. Her main interest is painting the big cats—tigers and lions—that are gradually vanishing from the earth due to poaching and loss of their native habitat. The detail and perfection of her work reflects her love for these animals. Her honors include many first place awards in the International Wildlife Art Show, and first place awards for three years in the Southeastern Wildlife Art Exhibit. In 1979, Ms. Keel was one of two artists who were the first women to do state duck stamps. And she is the first woman to have done a First of State duck stamp.

JIM KILLEN
1986 Vermont Duck Stamp

Jim Killen was born in Montevideo, Minnesota, on January 22, 1934. He ranks among the country's foremost wildlife artists, his memorable watercolors earning him acclaim wherever they are shown. After winning many awards and honors at art shows, Mr. Killen was presented the President's Award as the Outstanding Wildlife Artist of the Ducks Unlimited National Wildlife Art Show in Kansas City in 1980 and again in 1981. He was also commissioned by the Marshlands Fund, Inc., to design that organization's first annual stamp. He has done six winning state duck stamp designs for five states, and he was selected Ducks Unlimited Artist of the Year in 1984. Mr. Killen lives in rural Minnesota, where he manages the acreage surrounding his house for the wildlife which abounds there.

JOSEPH D. KNAP
1937–38 Federal Duck Stamp

Joseph D. Knap was born in Scottsdale, Pennsylvania, in 1875. His first business had always been real estate, with artwork a hobby, never a profession. At age forty-nine, at the insistence of one of his hunting companions, he first exhibited some of his watercolors at the Ackerman Galleries in New York. He met with almost immediate success. Mr. Knap preferred watercolor for most of his work, but he did make two sets of etchings, each set a limited edition of one hundred signed proofs for which the plates were destroyed after printing. In addition, Mr. Knap's paintings have been exhibited in many cities and were hung at the Grand Central Galleries and the American Museum of Natural History, both in New York. Mr. Knap died in 1962.

LESLIE C. KOUBA
1958–59 Federal Duck Stamp, 1967–68 Federal Duck Stamp

Leslie C. Kouba was born in Hutchinson, Minnesota, on February 3, 1917. He had an early interest in drawing and, at age fourteen, began taking art courses by correspondence from Art Instruction, Inc. These constituted the only formal art training he ever had, but they proved to be all he needed. In addition to being a respected wildlife artist, Mr. Kouba is also the founder and proprietor of one of the most respected art galleries of the country—the American Wildlife Art Galleries. This gallery represents some of the best work of the top artists of the nation in this field. Mr. Kouba has also met with success outside of his gallery, with his work in the form of prints achieving a wide distribution. Mr. Kouba has also spent much time photographing wildlife and traveling with Mrs. Kouba in search of Indian artifacts.

ROBERT KUSSEROW
1976 South Dakota Duck Stamp, 1985 Wyoming Duck Stamp

Robert Kusserow was born in Pennsylvania on September 2, 1929. He is a 1954 graduate of West Liberty State College, where he attained a Bachelor of Arts in fine arts. Until 1974, Mr. Kusserow was a commercial artist in Denver and also a biological illustrator for the University of Colorado. His works have appeared on several covers of the South Dakota *Conservation Digest* magazine. His paintings are noted for their characteristic attention to detail, and his exhibits across South Dakota have gained him recognition as one of the state's foremost wildlife artists. He now makes his home in Rapid City, South Dakota, where he has an art studio.

LEE LeBLANC
1973–74 Federal Duck Stamp, 1981 Arkansas Duck Stamp, 1981 South Carolina Duck Stamp

Lee LeBlanc was born in Powers, Michigan, on October 5, 1913. He received his formal training at the Frank Wiggins Trade School in Los Angeles, the LaFrance Art Institute in Philadelphia, the Art Students League in New York, the Chouinard School of Art and Jespen Art School in Los Angeles, plus private tutoring with Will Foster and Nicolai Fechin. Mr. LeBlanc worked for Western Lithographic as a commercial artist and as an artist and animator for Walt Disney Studios, 20th-Century Fox Studios, and MGM Studios. In 1962, he left film work to pursue a career as a freelance artist and returned to the only place he really could call home—Iron River, Michigan. Mr. LeBlanc is a member of Ducks Unlimited, the National Wildlife Federation, The Audubon Society, the National Geographic Society, the Ornithologists Union, and the Cornell Laboratory of Ornithology. He was the 1981 Deer Unlimited Artist of the Year.

ROBERT LESLIE
1987 Idaho Duck Stamp

Robert Leslie was born in Oconomowoc, Wisconsin, on August 8, 1947. He credits his love of the outdoors to his father and his artistic interests to his mother. His earliest exposure to wildlife was in the forests and marshes of Wisconsin, where he acquired the knowledge of natural habitats that can be seen in his paintings today. He was also a professional musician for twelve years and a recording artist for Motown Studios. He even entertained troops in Vietnam while on tour. It was only in 1985 that he launched his career as a wildlife artist. He decided to make art a full-time profession after competing in two shows and capturing first prize in each.

RONALD J. LOUQUE
1988 Virginia Duck Stamp

Ronald J. Louque was born in New Orleans, Louisiana, on March 3, 1952. He developed his interest in nature and wildlife through his school years, which led him to embark on a career in ornithology at Louisiana State University in 1970. It was there that he also discovered his talent for painting, and, although he received no formal instruction, in two years he was painting as a full-time professional artist. His works have appeared in several national publications, and he has won eight state stamp competitions. Mr. Louque also won the first annual World Painting Competition held in 1984 by the Ward Foundation in Maryland. He placed third in the 1986 Federal Duck Stamp competition. In addition, his works have been shown at many of the popular wildlife exhibits throughout the country.

DAVID A. MAASS
1974–75 Federal Duck Stamp, 1977 Minnesota Duck Stamp, 1982–83 Federal Duck Stamp, 1984 Maine Duck Stamp

David A. Maass was born in Rochester, New York, on November 27, 1929. He early developed a love of wildlife and began his career without any formal art education but with extraordinary native talent. He took a job as an illustrator with a manufacturer of high school and college jewelry, where he finally rose to the position of art director. In 1961, he became a full-time artist. By 1966, Mr. Maass' originals were selling so well that he began to produce limited-edition prints. He won the 1974 Ducks Unlimited Artist of the Year award. He holds this to be his proudest achievement because it comes from the votes of more than seven hundred Ducks Unlimited officers, conservationists, and hunters, all of whom know well the birds and habitats. His oil paintings and pencil sketches appear in Gene Long's book, *A Gallery of Waterfowl and Upland Birds*.

ALDERSON MAGEE
1976–77 Federal Duck Stamp

Alderson Magee was born in Hartford, Connecticut, on October 5, 1929. He began in industrial management with Pratt and Whitney Aircraft, but he always maintained an interest in painting and drawing. Finally, by 1971, he felt he could make it in the art world and retired from Pratt and Whitney. To improve his native talent, he enrolled in several courses at the Hartford Art League. There he studied with Estelle Coniff. In 1972, he decided to try the medium of scratchboard, which he had read about in an old artbook. He was fascinated by this technique and has used no other medium since.

NED MAYNE
1980 Delaware Duck Stamp

Ned Mayne grew up amidst the numerous creeks, rivers, and marshes of the Del-Mar-Va Peninsula near the Chesapeake Bay—one of the richest waterfowl wintering areas in the world. As a youngster he was interested in taxidermy and waterfowl hunting. From this, he gained his basic knowledge of waterfowl anatomy. Mr. Mayne received a Bachelor of Arts in art from the University of Delaware. He has won many awards at such events as the U.S. National Decoy Show at Babylon, New York, the Greater Goose Decoy Contest at Chincoteague, Virginia, and the Ward Foundation World Championships.

LAWRENCE K. MICHAELSEN
1979–80 Federal Duck Stamp

Lawrence K. ("Ken") Michaelsen was born in San Francisco on October 1, 1936. He has been painting ever since his childhood, when his father, an artist, was his mentor. After a hitch in the Air Force, he held a number of jobs in the commercial art world. It wasn't until the 1970s, though, that he started doing the wildlife paintings he is famous for today. It was in 1972 that a friend commissioned him to paint a Dall sheep, his first wildlife subject. After several other commissions to paint wildlife subjects, he knew he had found his niche and dropped out of commercial art for good. Mr. Michaelsen, in addition, is an accomplished photographer. He has taught classes at the Mendocino Art Center in the community where he and his wife, Judy, also an artist, reside.

GERALD MOBLEY
1985–86 Federal Duck Stamp

Gerald Mobley was born in Rector, Arkansas, on February 6, 1938. He has been an avid outdoorsman since his early years. While in the service, he worked on technical training aids for aircraft systems, and afterward went into commercial art, where he eventually founded his own now-successful commercial art studio in Tulsa. Since 1981, when he became seriously interested in wildlife art, he has spent most of his spare time at game preserves and zoos, photographing ducks and geese for reference material. Mr. Mobley separates his wildlife painting from his commercial work by painting wildlife subjects only in the studio in his home.

BURTON E. MOORE, JR.
1986–87 Federal Duck Stamp

Burton E. Moore, Jr., was born in Columbia, South Carolina, in 1945. A former Marine Corps captain, he is a self-taught artist and has made his living with his work since 1977. He is known nationally for outdoor scenes featuring sporting dogs, decoys, and waterfowl. His other honors include being selected as South Carolina Wildlife Federation Artist of the Year. Mr. Moore's works have been shown in galleries and at major exhibits throughout the nation. These include the Smithsonian Institution, the Cleveland Museum of Natural History, the Southeastern Wildlife Exposition, the Easton Waterfowl Festival, and the well-known Leigh Yawkey Woodson Art Museum Birds in Art Exhibition. A life sponsor of Ducks Unlimited, Mr. Moore resides in Charleston, South Carolina.

EDWARD A. MORRIS
1961–62 Federal Duck Stamp, 1962–63 Federal Duck Stamp

Edward A. Morris was born in Philadelphia on July 28, 1917. After eight years with the Marines, he studied at the Philadelphia College of Art, where two of his instructors were Henry C. Pitz and W. Emerton Heitland. Mr. Morris is a painter as well as an illustrator, and his work appears in many private collections. He shares with good wildlife artists a keen appreciation for the outdoors. His work has appeared in *Gopher Historian, Naturalist, Linn's Weekly Stamp News*, and other magazines. He was also a contributor to *The Northwestern Banks Hunting Guide* (1962). Over the years, his work has appeared in a wide variety of media: oil, watercolor, pen and ink, bronze, stone, lithography, drypoint etching, and ivory carving. He finds most interesting whatever he is working on at the moment.

WILLIAM C. MORRIS
1984–85 Federal Duck Stamp

William C. Morris was born in Mobile, Alabama, on June 8, 1945. He began sketching and enjoying the natural world around him during his early field trips as a young boy. Despite his interest in art, he studied engineering in college and joined Chevron Oil on graduation. On his own, he tried some watercolors, and one, a painting of football coach "Bear" Bryant, stirred up so much interest that he published a limited edition of a thousand prints. They sold out in four weeks and opened up a second career for him. Many of his original works are now in private collections. His two successes in 1984—the Federal and the Alabama Duck Stamp contests—will make his works even more highly prized by collectors.

MARTIN R. MURK
1977–78 Federal Duck Stamp

A native of Wisconsin, Martin R. Murk's wildlife art has earned him many awards, including the 1982 Wisconsin Wetlands for Wildlife Artist of the Year, 1984 Wisconsin Ducks Unlimited Artist of the Year, 1986 Wisconsin Waterfowler's Artist of the Year, and the 1987 Great Lakes Wildlife Artist of the Year. He is the winner of the 1977 Federal Duck Stamp competition, the 1979 Wisconsin Trout Stamp, and the 1980 Wisconsin Duck Stamp contest. Mr. Murk also designed Wisconsin's first Great Lakes Salmon and Trout Stamp and the first North American Endangered Species Conservation Stamp in 1982. Among the many places his work has been exhibited are the Great Lakes Wildlife Art Festival, National Wildlife Federation, Southeastern Wildlife Exposition, Waterfowl Festival, and the Leigh Yawkey Woodson Art Museum Birds in Art Exhibition. He is listed in *American Artists of Renown* and *Who's Who in Waterfowl Art* (1982).

JACK MURRAY
1947–48 Federal Duck Stamp

Jack Murray was born in Pittsburgh on August 12, 1889. He showed an early interest in sketching and taxidermy, and after graduation from Massachusetts State College in 1914, he completed his training at the Massachusetts School of Art. He went into the commercial art world and gradually got more and more assignments to do drawings and paintings for advertising agencies. He kept up with painting wildlife scenes as a hobby until the turning point in his career, when one of his wildlife paintings was published on the cover of the *Saturday Evening Post*. After that he was kept busy with magazine work, appearing in *Country Home, Better Homes and Gardens, Woman's Home Companion, Successful Farming, Good Housekeeping, Farmer's Wife, Boy's Life*, and others. Mr. Murray is deceased.

LEON PARSON
1986 Utah Waterfowl Stamp

Leon Parson was born in Provo, Utah, on May 13, 1951. He spent most of his life near Jackson Hole, Wyoming, close to Yellowstone Park—an ideal place for a wildlife artist. He was raised in a family that now counts five professional artists among its members, including his father. It is no surprise, then, that he began painting animals very early in life and is, today, primarily a big-game painter. His formal education includes a Bachelor of Fine Arts from the Art Center College of Design in Pasadena, California, and graduate study for his Master of Fine Arts in illustration from Syracuse University in New York. His works have appeared on the covers of such magazines as *Outdoor Life, Petersen's Hunting, North American Hunter*, and others. Mr. Parson lives in Rexburg, Idaho, with his wife and family.

CARROLL J. AND GWEN K. PERKINS
1976 Mississippi Duck Stamp

Carroll J. and Gwen K. Perkins, husband and wife naturalists, submitted their winning photograph for the 1976 Mississippi Duck Stamp competition jointly. Dr. Perkins was born in Leesville, Louisiana, on May 21, 1915. Dr. Gwen Kirtley Perkins was born in Marlow, Oklahoma, on March 23, 1918. Mr. Perkins has retired from a professorship in Wildlife Management at the School of Forest Resources, Mississippi State University. Their photographs have appeared in numerous national publications under the credit Kirtley-Perkins.

RICHARD W. PLASSCHAERT
1980–81 Federal Duck Stamp, 1982 North Dakota Duck Stamp, 1983 New Hampshire Duck Stamp, 1983 North Carolina Duck Stamp

Richard W. Plasschaert was born in New Ulm, Minnesota, on April 25, 1941. Very soon he realized that he possessed a special ability to capture the beauty of nature in painting. His art, however, does not always reflect his lifelong interest in wildlife, much of it comprising landscapes and portraits. Mr. Plasschaert has spent over twenty-five years in the fields of commercial art, layout and design, portrait, landscape, and wildlife painting. He is skilled in the use of oils, acrylics, and watercolors. Most of his paintings have sold well in the New York market; additionally, he received a great honor when he was accepted into the National Academy. His work, both originals and prints, can be found in many of the nation's galleries.

ROGER E. PREUSS
1949–50 Federal Duck Stamp

Roger E. Preuss was born in Waterville, Minnesota, on January 22, 1922. After service in the Naval Reserve he attended the Minneapolis College of Art. When he was only twenty-six, he won the Federal Duck Stamp contest; he is the youngest artist to date ever to have won the competition. He has also won twenty-one national and international juried art honors. His paintings have been exhibited in twenty leading art museums, including the Joslyn Art Museum and the Institute of Contemporary Arts. He was elected a Fellow by the International Institute of Arts and Letters and Vice President by the Wildlife Artists of the World. Mr. Preuss is also a member of the Society of Animal Artists. He is the author of *Outdoor Horizons*, and his work has appeared in sixty-five national magazines. Named United States Bicentennial Wildlife Artist in 1976, Mr. Preuss is listed in thirty of the world's standard references, including Marquis's *Who's Who in the World*.

CLAREMONT GALE PRITCHARD
1968–69 Federal Duck Stamp

Claremont Gale ("Bud") Pritchard was born in Kenesaw, Nebraska, on June 18, 1910. His formal art training took the form of correspondence courses, and he received certificates from the Washington School of Art and later from the Federal School of Art, now Art Instruction Schools, of Minneapolis. He served in World War II and, back in civilian life, he gained increasing artistic recognition. At the Nebraska Game and Parks Commission, his chief responsibility was illustrating that agency's *Outdoor Nebraska*. At the same time, he did illustrations for *The Pronghorn Antelope*, *Animal Behavior*, and *Mammals of North America*. Moreover, he exhibited throughout the country. He was a charter member of the Audubon Naturalists' Club in Lincoln, Nebraska. Mr. Pritchard is deceased.

MAYNARD REECE
1948–49 Federal Duck Stamp, 1951–52 Federal Duck Stamp, 1959–60 Federal Duck Stamp, 1969–70 Federal Duck Stamp, 1971–72 Federal Duck Stamp, 1972 Iowa Duck Stamp

Maynard Reece was born in Arnolds Park, Iowa, in 1920. His love of nature combined with undeniable artistic talent have made him one of America's foremost wildlife painters. He began drawing at an early age and won his first award in 1932 when he was twelve years old. After finishing school, he went into commercial art and then joined the Iowa Museum in Des Moines, where he stayed for ten years interrupted by World War II. In 1951, he turned to freelancing and has been a full-time artist ever since. He has won the Federal Duck Stamp contest an unprecedented *five* times, and in all he has a total of twenty-two stamp designs to his credit. Mr. Reece's works have appeared in many museums, books, and publications, and they are now in such demand that most of his paintings are sold even before they are completed.

ALDEN LASSELL RIPLEY
1942–43 Federal Duck Stamp

Alden Lassell Ripley was born in Wakefield, Massachusetts, on December 31, 1896. After serving abroad in World War I, he returned to a scholarship at the Museum of Fine Arts in Boston. He completed his studies there and was granted a fellowship for two years of study in Europe. Shortly after his return, he held an exhibition of his watercolors and was made a member of the Guild of Boston Artists. His murals and etchings are well known and widely respected. Two famous murals of his are "Purchase of the Land from the Indians" and "Paul Revere's Ride." His paintings are found in many noted galleries and in private collections as well. Mr. Ripley was a member of a number of artistic societies, and was elected to the National Academy of Design, a distinction generally considered to be the highest an artist in the United States can attain. Mr. Ripley died in 1969.

JOHN A. RUTHVEN
1960–61 Federal Duck Stamp, 1982 Ohio Duck Stamp

John A. Ruthven was born in Cincinnati, Ohio, on November 12, 1924. After serving in the Navy during World War II, he attended the Art Academy in Cincinnati. In 1946, he started his own commercial art studio which he turned over to his employees in 1959. In 1961, he won the Federal Duck Stamp competition. By the time he was forty, Mr. Ruthven had achieved a national reputation as a naturalist and as an animal and bird artist. Among his many achievements, Mr. Ruthven painted the American Bald Eagle unveiled at a reception held in his honor in the East Room of the White House in 1976. He was the first Ducks Unlimited Artist of the Year, is a member of the Society of Animal Artists of New York City, and is a trustee of the Cincinnati Museum of Natural History.

HARVEY DEAN SANDSTROM
1954–55 Federal Duck Stamp

Harvey Dean Sandstrom was born in St. Paul, Minnesota, in 1925. In 1946, after serving in the Navy in World War II, he began four years of study at the Minneapolis School of Art. He then did freelance commercial artwork in Duluth, Minnesota, and began an art studio with three partners. It was also at this time that Mr. Sandstrom began painting wildlife in earnest. He held several one-man shows and displayed and sold original paintings in sporting goods stores and galleries in New York, Chicago, and other locations in the East, South, and Midwest. Inspiration from a hunting trip near Grand Rapids, Minnesota, led to the ring-necked duck design that later appeared as his winning entry in the Federal Duck Stamp competition.

PATRICK SAWYER
1980 Oklahoma Duck Stamp

Patrick Sawyer was born on August 5, 1948. Part of his experience with and understanding of wildlife comes from his nine years in Alaska working as a wildlife artist. Mr. Sawyer's works have been exhibited at the National Wildlife Art Show in Kansas City, the Safari Club, the Anchorage Audubon Show, and the Oklahoma Wildlife Art Show in Tulsa. He has works in collections of Remington Arms, Winchester Press, and *Outdoor Oklahoma* magazine. Mr. Sawyer was selected to do the 1986 Oklahoma Ducks Unlimited Sponsor print.

PHIL SCHOLER
1983–84 Federal Duck Stamp

Phil Scholer was born in Rochester, Minnesota, on July 7, l951. He developed an early love of nature from childhood camping trips with his family, and after high school, he enrolled in the Mankato State University College of Fine Arts. He supported himself with various jobs while trying freelance work, and he was on the verge of going freelance full-time when he won the Federal Duck Stamp contest. He was not always a wildlife painter; he worked on portraits and landscapes in college and for a time thereafter. One day he saw a painting by another local artist, David Maass, and was very impressed by the way Maass incorporated birds into his landscape. New horizons opened to him and his career in wildlife painting was born. He has continued to develop as one of the country's most talented waterfowl artists.

CHARLES W. SCHWARTZ
1979 Missouri Duck Stamp

Charles W. Schwartz was born on June 2, 1914, in St. Louis, Missouri. He was commissioned by the Missouri Department of Conservation to design Missouri's initial state duck stamp. Mr. Schwartz has worked for nearly forty years in the Department as an artist, photographer, and writer. He is a biologist by academic training, receiving Bachelor of Arts, Master of Arts, and Doctor of Science degrees from the University of Missouri. He has written several award-winning scientific books and has produced some twenty-five motion pictures on wildlife, all of which have received national or international awards.

CLAYTON B. SEAGEARS
1953–54 Federal Duck Stamp

Clayton B. Seagears was born in 1897. At the University of Michigan, he majored in zoology and journalism. After a stint of teaching at the University, he spent the next thirteen years, 1924 to 1937, in newspaper work, including cartooning. Mr. Seagears was a self-taught artist. He did general commercial work and later specialized in outdoor and wildlife subjects. He founded *The Conservationist*, the official publication of New York State's Conservation Department; most of his work was done for that journal until his retirement from the Department in 1962. His illustrations and writings have appeared in many books and publications. He worked mostly in tempera, specializing in birds with an emphasis on waterfowl and upland game. Mr. Seagears died in 1983.

MICHAEL SIEVE
1984 Oregon Duck Stamp

Michael Sieve was born in Wilmont, Minnesota, on September 2, 1951. He was raised in what was once known as the pheasant hunting capital of Minnesota. He spent much time as a youth hunting and fishing in southwestern Minnesota, Iowa, and northwestern Colorado, and he began drawing wildlife long before starting school. He studied art at Southern Minnesota State College in Marshall. Relying heavily on first-hand experience as the inspiration and basis for his painting, Mr. Sieve travels extensively and frequently to all parts of Canada, Alaska, the northern and western United States, and Central America. Although accomplished in many media, he prefers oils and specializes in big game subjects. He has exhibited in the Minnesota Wildlife Heritage Show and the Leigh Yawkey Woodson Birds in Art Exhibition.

DANIEL SMITH

1985 Alaska Duck Stamp, 1985 Georgia Duck Stamp, 1987 Arizona Duck Stamp, 1987 West Virginia Duck Stamp, 1988–89 Federal Duck Stamp

Daniel Smith was born in Mankato, Minnesota, on August 1, 1954. Before devoting his life full-time to wildlife art, he spent eight years in the commercial art field as an illustrator. This experience broadened and deepened his technique and contributed greatly to his unique style—a style that has brought him widespread recognition. He won first-of-state selections for stamp designs in Alaska and Georgia in 1985. He won the 1986 South Carolina waterfowl contest, and he was also selected to design the First of State New Mexico Turkey Stamp and the First of State Arizona Waterfowl Stamp. His works have been selected for the Leigh Yawkey Woodson Art Museum Birds in Art Exhibition, and he continues to participate each year in the Minnesota Wildlife Heritage Show. He resides with his family near Eden Prairie, Minnesota.

NED SMITH

1983 Pennsylvania Duck Stamp

Ned Smith was born on October 9, 1919, in Millerburg, Pennsylvania, where he was introduced to the natural world of the Susquehanna Valley and its surrounding fields and mountains by his father, an avid botanist and outdoorsman. Mr. Smith, besides his talent with a brush, was also a naturalist, illustrator, and talented writer. He designed stamps for the Raptor Fund, the Pennsylvania Federation of Sportsman Clubs, the Pennsylvania Turkey Federation, and the National Wild Turkey Federation.

STANLEY STEARNS

1955–56 Federal Duck Stamp, 1964–65 Federal Duck Stamp, 1966–67 Federal Duck Stamp

Stanley Stearns was born in Washington, D.C., on January 15, 1926. He spent much of his childhood in Hawaii, where his father was a geologist. He attended high school in Hawaii and Seattle, college in Seattle, and served in the Marine Corps in World War II. After the war, he attended the Vesper George School of Art and the Massachusetts School of Art in Boston, receiving training in both commercial and fine art. For some years, he worked full-time at commercial technical art, confining his painting and sculpture to the weekends. He did landscapes, city scenes, figures, and portraits, using various media. As time went by, though, he turned more and more to wildlife subjects. His first sale of wildlife art was a group of "spots" for *American Rifleman*. Mr. Stearns's work is in numerous public and private collections throughout the country.

JOHN W. TAYLOR

1974 Maryland Duck Stamp

John W. Taylor was born in Washington, D.C., on April 19, 1931. He began an avid interest in birds when his fourth-grade teacher formed a Junior Audubon Club. The idea of bird painting as a profession did not develop until he started work for the Division of Birds at the U.S. National Museum in Washington where a close association with artists and ornithologists formed the basis and inspiration for his life's work. After service in the military, he returned to the Museum and studied art and design at the Corcoran Gallery School in Washington, D.C. After that he had a position as an artist and editor with the Maryland Department of Game and Fisheries. Mr. Taylor has been freelancing since 1965. In 1985, 1986, and 1987 he designed conservation nongame stamps for Maryland.

JOE THORNBRUGH

1986 Montana Waterfowl Stamp

Joe Thornbrugh was born in Blackwell, Oklahoma, on June 24, 1948. His lifelong interest in wildlife and the outdoors was developed during his childhood in western Montana, where he has spent many years painting and sketching the local flora and fauna. Birds, however, are his most frequent subject. He works in acrylics, taking great pains to capture the brilliant colors and intricate designs of the birds' plumage. Mr. Thornbrugh's works have appeared in many national shows and in the Leigh Yawkey Woodson Art Museum. He lives in Victor, Montana, with his wife and family.

OSCAR WARBACH

1976 Michigan Duck Stamp

Oscar Warbach was born in Elizabeth, New Jersey, in 1913. After receiving a Bachelor of Science from Rutgers University and a Bachelor of Science in zoology from Michigan State University, he joined the Michigan Department of Conservation in 1941. After the war years, Mr. Warbach returned to the Michigan Department of Conservation and stayed there until 1948, when he became a research biologist for the U.S. Fish and Wildlife Service at the Patuxent Research Center in Laurel, Maryland. In 1954, he returned to the Michigan Department of Conservation, now the Department of Natural Resources, and remained there as an illustrator and biologist until retiring in 1977.

KEITH WARRICK

1986 Washington Duck Stamp

Keith Warrick was born in Preston, Idaho, on February 7, 1938. He is a self-taught artist who received his only formal art training at the University of Washington, as a commercial artist. He is recognized as one of the West's most talented wildlife artists, and his works have appeared in numerous national publications and have been shown in galleries throughout the country. He has also designed the 1980 Washington Upland Game Bird Stamp, the 1981 and 1983 Washington Salmon Stamps, the 1986 First of State Washington Migratory Duck Stamp, and the 1985 through 1987 Ducks Unlimited Artist of the Year Print for Washington State. Mr. Warrick resides in Lake Stevens, Washington.

WALTER A. WEBER

1944–45 Federal Duck Stamp, 1950–51 Federal Duck Stamp

Walter A. Weber was born in Chicago on May 23, 1906. He received all his formal education there and worked there for several years after college. He attended the Chicago Art Institute, the American Academy of Art, and the Church School of Art. Trained as a scientific illustrator, he joined the Chicago Field Museum, now the Chicago Museum of Natural History, in 1928. He traveled extensively for the museum on field trips throughout the world. In the mid-1930s, Mr. Weber turned to freelance artwork, which he continued until 1949, when he went on staff as artist and naturalist for the National Geographic Society. In 1967, he was awarded the highest civilian honor the U.S. Department of the Interior can bestow—the Conservation Service Award. Mr. Weber died on January 10, 1979.

MILTON C. WEILER

1974 Massachusetts Duck Stamp

Milton C. Weiler graduated from the Syracuse College of Fine Arts and took up the painting of portraits. After a year he entered the teaching profession. From 1935 until his death, he was associated with the Garden City Public School system as head of the Fine and Industrial Arts Department. His watercolors of wildlife have the authenticity of an artist who has lived the life he has painted. An outdoorsman and conservationist, he was devoted to trout and salmon fishing, waterfowl, and upland gunning. While he worked as a teacher, his work graced some of the Derrydale titles on gunning and fishing, and some other publishers' books as well, including Scribner's, Coward-McCann, Stackpole, and Winchester Press. Mr. Weiler died in 1974.

JOHN S. WILSON

1981–82 Federal Duck Stamp, 1986 South Dakota Waterfowl Restoration Stamp

John S. Wilson was born in Sisseton, South Dakota, on June 6, 1929. Many of his boyhood days were spent hunting and fishing, activities he still enjoys and which help him gain first-hand knowledge for his wildlife paintings. He attended school in Sisseton and then enlisted in the Air Force in 1946. Returning to civilian life in 1954, he studied architectural drafting for a year and then worked as a designer and artist for a sign company for twenty-five years. For Mr. Wilson, painting was a hobby to be practiced on his own time. He did not paint any wildlife subjects until 1976, when he entered the state's duck stamp contest, taking second place. Fired with enthusiasm, he went on to win the 1981 South Dakota Pheasant and the 1981 Federal Duck Stamp contests.